MODERN WORLD NATIONS

Mexico
Second Edition

Charles F. Gritzner
South Dakota State University

CHELSEA HOUSE
An Infobase Learning Company

Frontispiece: Flag of Mexico

Cover: Playa del Carmen, Mexico

Mexico, Second Edition

Copyright © 2011 by Infobase Learning

All rights reserved. No part of this book may be reproduced or utilized in any form or by any means, electronic or mechanical, including photocopying, recording, or by any information storage or retrieval systems, without permission in writing from the publisher. For information, contact:

Chelsea House
An imprint of Infobase Learning
132 West 31st Street
New York, NY 10001

Library of Congress Cataloging-in-Publication Data
Gritzner, Charles F.
 Mexico / Charles F. Gritzner. — 2nd ed.
  p. cm. — (Modern world nations)
 Includes bibliographical references and index.
 ISBN 978-1-60413-938-9 (hardcover : acid-free paper) 1. Mexico—Juvenile literature. I. Title.
 F1208.5.G75 2011
 972—dc22
                                2010036237

Chelsea House books are available at special discounts when purchased in bulk quantities for businesses, associations, institutions, or sales promotions. Please call our Special Sales Department in New York at (212) 967-8800 or (800) 322-8755.

You can find Chelsea House on the World Wide Web at
http://www.chelseahouse.com

Text design by Takeshi Takahashi
Cover design by Alicia Post
Composition by EJB Publishing Services
Cover printed by Yurchak Printing, Landisville, Penn.
Book printed and bound by Yurchak Printing, Landisville, Penn.
Date printed: April 2011
Printed in the United States of America

10 9 8 7 6 5 4 3 2 1

This book is printed on acid-free paper.

All links and Web addresses were checked and verified to be correct at the time of publication. Because of the dynamic nature of the Web, some addresses and links may have changed since publication and may no longer be valid.

Table of Contents

Mexico

Second Edition

Mexico presents many contrasts between traditional and contemporary lifestyles. While Mexico City boasts all the modern offerings of a large urban center, remote villages whose inhabitants maintain traditional customs dot the landscape.

1

Introducing Northern America's Southern Neighbor

When you think about Mexico, what comes to mind? What mental pictures do you have of its physical environment? What images do you see of the country's people and their way of life? How important do you think Mexico is to *norteamericanos* (Northern Americans, or residents of the United States and Canada), to other Latin American countries, and to the rest of the world?

Take a moment to mentally list any five things that you think are typical of Mexico. Does your list include small, sleepy villages with mud huts and dusty streets? Or possibly poor farmers, wearing huge sombreros, plodding along beside their burros? Perhaps it includes a parched desert with searing heat and cacti standing like lonely sentinels with raised arms. Not surprisingly, these are images held by many Anglo-Americans who are unfamiliar with their southern neighbor.

The foregoing images are mainly stereotypes—overly simplified beliefs that are untrue, or are greatly exaggerated. *Some* of these images can be found in present-day Mexico. The country offers a wonderful contrast of traditional life (folk culture) and contemporary living (popular culture). Such false images or beliefs, often instilled by the media, can and do influence the way places are viewed. In a closely knit global community, it is essential to understand our global neighbors. This is particularly true of Mexico and its approximately 113 million citizens with whom the United States shares its southern border. It is often said that there are "many Mexicos." Its natural environment offers a spectacular diversity of features and conditions. And its people represent a complex mosaic of physical features and cultures (ways of living).

AN EMERGING GIANT

Mexico—officially the *Estados Unidos Mexicanos* (United Mexican States)—is an emerging giant. Its area of about 760,000 square miles (1,970,000 square kilometers) occupies nearly 70 percent of Middle America. The country's large and rapidly growing population of about 113 million ranks third in the Western Hemisphere (behind the United States and Brazil) and eleventh in the world. Among Western Hemisphere countries, Mexico ranks fourth in area (behind Canada, the United States, and Brazil). The country is a growing economic giant. Its gross domestic product (GDP) is outstripped in the Americas only by those of the United States and Brazil. Many international organizations and businesses recognize Mexico's importance. Today, in global affairs, the country is often included with its neighbors, the United States and Canada, rather than with the other Latin American nations.

Mexicans take great pride in their country's many achievements. The following list includes some interesting rankings and facts about the country and its people.

- Mexico's population ranks eleventh in the world.

- The country's economy is the third greatest in the Western Hemisphere and ranks twelfth in the world.

- Mexico has more Spanish-speaking people than any other country.

- Depending upon the definition of "metropolitan area," Mexico City is the world's third-largest city.

- More American Indians live in Mexico than in any other country.

- Mexico has the world's largest pyramid, the Pyramid of the Sun at Teotihuacán.

- Mexican salsa has passed ketchup as Anglo-America's favorite condiment.

- Mexico City is home to the Western Hemisphere's oldest university, founded in 1551.

- Mexico has the two largest universities in the Western Hemisphere.

- Mexican music is the fastest growing in popularity in the United States.

- Mexico City's archaeological museum is recognized as being one of the world's finest.

- Mexico City has the second-largest subway system in the Americas.

- Mexico's Barranca Cobre (Copper Canyon) is larger than Arizona's Grand Canyon.

- Mexico is the primary tourist destination for U.S. citizens.

- Mexicans are the fastest-growing ethnic group in the United States; by 2050, it is estimated that "Garcia" will replace "Smith" as the most common surname in the country.

- Mexico City is the highest large city in North America.

SORTING OUT REGIONS

Geographers divide the lands and peoples of the Americas into many regions. North America and South America are continents. The Isthmus of Panama—the narrow strip of land through which the Panama Canal was cut—is the dividing point between the continents. Mexico lies entirely in North America. Latin America and Anglo-America are cultural regions based on language and way of life. Latin America, of which Mexico is a part, includes all Western Hemisphere countries settled by the Spanish or Portuguese peoples. Northern America includes predominantly English-speaking Canada and the United States. The boundary between the two regions is the U.S.-Mexico border. Middle America is the region within Latin America that includes all countries between the United States and the continent of South America, including Mexico, the islands of the Caribbean, and Central America. Mexico is the largest country of Middle America. Mesoamerica is a term archaeologists and anthropologists use in reference to that part of Middle America that was home to well-developed early civilizations. Finally, there is Central America, the area of mainland North America that lies south of Mexico and north of South America.

A VARIED NATURAL LANDSCAPE

Mexico is a country of great physical contrasts. Huge, snow-clad volcanic peaks near Mexico City contrast sharply with the flat, almost featureless tropical plains of the Yucatán Peninsula. Much of the country is rugged plateau. In places, rivers have

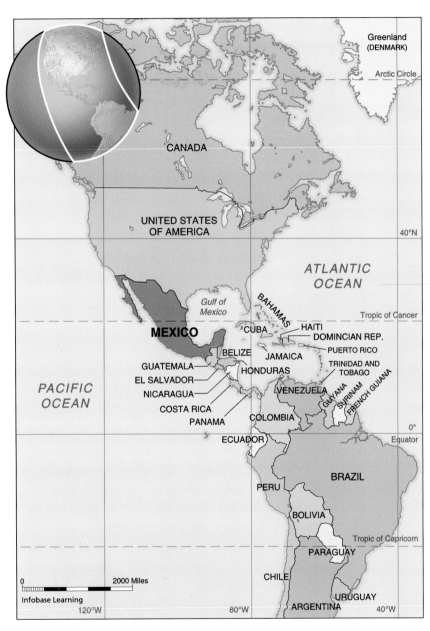

Mexico is the southern neighbor of the United States. It is the northernmost country of the Latin America culture region and the largest country of Middle America. Both the Pacific and Atlantic oceans bathe its shores. The country's southern extreme borders the Central American republics of Guatemala and Belize.

scoured huge canyons, called *barrancas*. The country's rugged features make farming and travel difficult in many places.

Climate and vegetation, too, offer great contrasts. Mexico's northern deserts are much like those of the bordering south-western United States. Parched desert landscapes stretch for hundreds of miles. Yet in southern Mexico, hot, wet conditions support a dense tropical forest. Higher peaks in central Mexico remain snow covered throughout the year.

Mineral wealth has been a key to Mexico's historical and economic development. During the colonial period, rich silver deposits made Mexico the world's major producer of this precious metal. During the last half of the twentieth century, Mexico became a major producer of petroleum.

In terms of its natural environment, Mexico offers many opportunities and presents many challenges. Chapter 2 discusses in greater detail the country's land, ecosystems, and natural resources.

A RICH NATIVE HISTORY

Few countries in the world have a native history as diverse, or as advanced, as that of Mexico. The region was one of the world's most important centers of early cultural growth and development. Thousands of years ago, native peoples were raising crops. Many of these crops, such as corn (maize), beans, squash, and peppers, remain important today. Elaborate systems of terracing and irrigation were built to make the land more productive. With abundant food, people began living in cities, including two that were among the largest urban centers in the world at the time. Before the Spanish conquerors arrived, Mexico's native culture—including its agriculture, astronomy, art, architecture, and science—was in many ways as highly developed as that of Europe at the time.

LASTING SPANISH IMPRINT

In 1521 a small group of Spaniards conquered the vast and powerful Aztec empire and changed Mexico forever. Spaniards

Mexico is a travel destination because of its open spaces, varied climates, beautiful scenery, and diverse people.

soon began to leave their own cultural imprint on the native landscape and practices. Today, the Spanish language, Spanish-introduced religion and customs, and Spanish-influenced economic and political practices dominate Mexican culture.

MANY MEXICOS

Today, Mexico is struggling to gain a foothold among the world's leading nations. Progress is often slow, and many Mexican people are impatient. The country's agriculture and industry have not been able to keep pace with its booming

Outdoor markets provide the rural population with a place to barter for goods and to socialize.

population. Chapter 5 in this journey through Mexico pauses to view the country's population and settlements—its rural villages and huge modern cities. Socially and economically, there continues to be a huge gap between the very rich and the extremely poor. The country is still working to achieve true democracy.

As Mexico is presented through the eyes of a geographer, be on the lookout for certain things. Watch for strengths that can help Mexico grow in power and influence. Search for factors or conditions that can weaken Mexico by causing conflicts or can otherwise hinder progress in some way. And of greatest importance, try to recognize ways in which Mexico—its people and its culture (way of life)—is becoming increasingly important to the United States.

Enjoy your journey through Mexico. Have an interesting, exciting, and enjoyable learning adventure. *¡Viva Mexico!* (Long live Mexico!)

The Gulf of California separates Baja California from Mexico's mainland. Beaches such as this with sand and rocks can be found in the Pacific coast area.

CHAPTER

2

Land of Environmental Diversity

"**D**iverse," "fantastic variety," and "great extremes" are just some of the terms used by writers to describe Mexico's many physical environments. Few countries on Earth can match the variety of physical features found in Mexico.

Geography is unique among the sciences. It serves as a bridge of understanding that links humans to Earth's natural environments. To be able to understand people—where they live, how they use Earth's elements, what they do, and what natural challenges they must overcome—it is important to know something about the physical conditions of the places they occupy. This chapter discusses Mexico's land features, climate and vegetation, natural resources, natural hazards, and other important natural elements. See how each of them has presented Mexico and its people with both opportunities and obstacles. Discover how people have lived in, used, and changed their natural environment over thousands of years.

SIZE AND SHAPE

Mexico's area of about 760,000 square miles (1.97 million square km) is roughly equal to the combined area of California, Arizona, New Mexico, Oklahoma, and Texas. As is true of these southwestern states, Mexico also has desert, rugged mountains, broad plateaus, deep canyons, and rolling plains. The country is widest in the north, where it spans a distance of about 1,300 miles (2,092 km) from the Pacific Ocean to the Gulf of Mexico. Its land narrows as the country stretches in a southeasterly direction to the Isthmus of Tehuantepec. Here, the land narrows to a strip about 140 miles (225 km) wide. Farther east, the land extends as a narrow mountainous "backbone" toward Central America.

Two pieces of land jut out to form large peninsulas. In the west, Baja California reaches nearly 750 miles (1,207 km) southward into the Pacific Ocean. This narrow finger of land is separated from mainland Mexico by the Gulf of California. The Yucatán Peninsula forms the country's easternmost area. This flat, low-lying plain extends some 250 miles (402 km) northward into the Gulf of Mexico. It is bordered on the east by the tropical waters of the Caribbean Sea.

LANDFORMS

Most of Mexico's land is rugged. Nearly three-fourths of the country lies at an elevation above 2,000 feet (609 meters). Less than 15 percent of its area is flat, and nearly all of the plains are found on the hot, relatively dry Yucatán Peninsula. Just over 10 percent of the country is well suited to farming.

Mountains

Mexico's mountain ranges resemble the letter "Y." The western arm of the "Y" is formed by the Sierra Madre Occidental

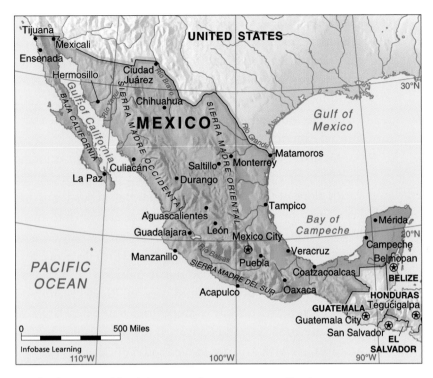

Mexico is a rugged land that extends some 2,000 miles (3,200 kilometers) in a northwesterly to southeasterly direction. Its 760,000-square-mile (1,970,000-square-kilometer) area includes hot desert landscapes in the north, a high central plateau that is home to most Mexican people and economic activity, and tropical mountains and lowland plains in the south and southeast.

(Mother Mountain Range of the West), which extends southward from Mexico's border with Arizona and New Mexico. The mountains and their many canyons form a huge barrier to east–west travel. A century ago, no road or railroad crossed the mountains for a distance of more than 750 miles (1,207 km). Even today, no road crosses northern sections of this rugged range for a stretch of more than 300 miles (483 km). Throughout Mexico, most highways and railroads parallel, rather than cross, the mountains.

The Sierra Madre Oriental (Mother Mountain Range of the East) extends southward from near the border with New Mexico and Texas, forming the eastern arm of the "Y." Both ranges join just south of Mexico City and continue southward, forming the eastward-bending stem of the "Y," which forms the mountainous backbone of southern Mexico and Central America.

Mexico's mountains offer spectacular scenery, including deep canyons and towering, snow-capped volcanic peaks. The Pacific slope of the Sierra Madre Occidental, in particular, has been sliced by millions of years of water erosion into many huge canyons, or barrancas. One of them, Barranca Cobre (Copper Canyon), is nearly 5,000 feet (1,524 m) deep and covers an area of more than 6,000 square miles, or 15,540 square kilometers (about the combined area of Rhode Island and Connecticut). The canyon is deeper and four times larger in area than Arizona's Grand Canyon. It is also the largest wilderness area in North America located south of Canada.

The canyon is home to nearly 50,000 Tarahumara Indians. Some anthropologists believe that these are the most primitive people in North America. In their very remote, nearly inaccessible location, ideas from the outside world hardly ever reach them. Because of their isolation, visiting the few villages in the canyon is like taking a step back in time. Not until 1961 was their area linked to the outside world. In that year, a railroad was completed through the canyon linking Chihuahua and the coastal city of Los Mochis. As the railroad winds through the deep gorge, it passes through 90 tunnels and crosses nearly 30 bridges.

Southern and western Mexico lie within a huge geologic zone often called the Pacific Ring (or Rim) of Fire. This rim of geologic instability surrounds much of the Pacific Ocean basin and is formed by the moving edges of several tectonic plates. Approximately 80 percent of all the world's volcanic and earthquake activity occur within this narrow, horseshoe-shaped zone—and Mexico receives its share of both.

Volcanoes

Mexico is home to some of the world's largest, most spectacular, and most active volcanoes. Volcanoes were held sacred by the peoples of ancient Mexico. Now, as then, volcanoes are viewed with awe, respect, and often fear by people living in their shadows. The country's highest peak is the mighty Mount Orizaba. This snow-capped, 18,406-foot (5,610-m) volcanic giant is the third-highest mountain in North America. Most volcanic activity occurs in an area reaching from Mexico City southward. This huge capital city, in fact, is surrounded on three sides by a high wall of volcanoes—including Iztaccíhuatl and Popocatépetl, both of which rise to more than 17,000 feet (5,182 m). Several of Mexico's volcanoes have been active in recent years. Unfortunately, they are located in densely populated areas, and they pose a great threat to human life and property.

Certainly one of Mexico's, if not the world's, most famous volcanic peaks is Mount Paricutín. One morning in 1943, a farmer named Dionisio Pulido was plowing his field near San Juan, a small town located some 180 miles (290 km) west of Mexico City. Plodding along behind his yoke (team) of oxen, he suddenly noticed a strange odor. Imagine his shock when he saw a thin column of smoke spiraling upward from a small hole in his field! Not knowing what to do, he covered the hole with a rock and continued plowing.

Soon, he noticed even more smoke coming from the ground. Startled by this strange sight, he ran to the village to tell the priest and townspeople what was happening in his field. Many people returned to the field with him to see this strange event for themselves. When they arrived, a hole nearly 30 feet (9 m) deep had formed. This gaping monster was now belching dense black clouds of foul-smelling smoke.

That night, a violent explosion shook the village, and a mountain began to rise from the field that Señor Pulido had been plowing only hours earlier. Within one week, the mountain had reached a height of 560 feet (171 m). Two months later, it had grown to nearly 1,000 feet (305 m) and was still growing. Today, a 1,300-foot-high (396-meter-high) volcanic cinder cone—Mount Paricutín—rises above the field in which corn once grew.

El Chicón is a large volcanic peak located in the state of Chiapas just east of the Isthmus of Tehuantepec. In 1982, the mountain erupted violently, spewing huge clouds of ash high into the atmosphere. Scientists believe that the volcanic ash shaded Earth from some of the sun's rays, causing temperatures worldwide to be 2° to 3°F (0.5 to 1.5°C) cooler for several years.

"El Popo," as Mexicans call the giant Mount Popocatépetl, rises to an elevation of 17,887 feet (5,452 m). It is one of the tallest active volcanoes in the world. Unfortunately, it is also located in one of the world's most densely populated areas. More than 25 million people, including most residents of Mexico City, live within 40 miles (64 km) of the volcanic peak. Recently, El Popo has shown increasing activity. During the late 1990s, the volcano once again began living up to its Aztec name—"Smoking Mountain." It experienced several rather violent eruptions, sending huge clouds of smoke and ash thousands of feet into the atmosphere.

There is reason to fear Popocatépetl. Three things could happen that would devastate vast areas, two of which could take a terrible toll on human lives. First, an eruption of gas, dust, and ash (such as that of the late 1990s) could change Earth's temperature for several years and also bury surrounding areas in gritty ash. A second type of event, a blast of hot lava and ash, would melt glaciers and snow on the mountain's northern slope. This would cause lahars, or mudflows, that would race down the mountain and into the surrounding valley, destroying everything in their path. Finally, some scientists

Active volcanoes are common in Mexico. Mount Popocatépetl billows ash and steam into the towns at its base. Violent eruptions can cause enormous damage to the countryside.

fear a more violent eruption, similar to the 1981 massive blast of Mount Saint Helens in Washington State. In such a densely populated area, were this kind of violent eruption to occur, it could kill millions of people and destroy billions of dollars' worth of property.

Much of western and southern Mexico also lies on fault zones that spawn severe earthquakes. Nearly all places located on the half of Mexico facing the Pacific Ocean have experienced destructive tremors. Many communities have been struck on numerous occasions. In 1985, a violent earthquake struck the heart of Mexico City. More than 10,000 people were killed, hundreds of thousands of families were left homeless, and the devastation caused billions of dollars' worth of property losses.

Plateau

A high plateau separates the Sierra Madre Oriental and Sierra Madre Occidental. This tableland is lower in the north, near Mexico's largest river, the Rio Grande (called the Rio Bravo in Mexico), which forms the border between Texas and Mexico. The plateau gradually rises in elevation as it stretches in a southeasterly direction toward Mexico City. There, in the Valley of Mexico, it reaches an elevation of more than 8,000 feet (2,438 m) near Mexico City. This area is the heart of Mexico. It holds nearly half of the country's population and a good portion of its social, political, and economic activity. Yet it lies at an elevation nearly half a mile (805 m) higher than the highest large city in the United States, "Mile High" Denver, Colorado.

How can there be a plateau with no steep downward slopes? And how is it possible to have a "valley" located on a high plateau? A plateau is defined as an area of nearly flat land bordered on several sides by steep slopes. Steep slopes border Mexico's huge Central Plateau—but they are steep mountain slopes that rise upward. The Valley of Mexico occupies the southern end of the Mexican Plateau, but it is surrounded on three sides by mountains that rise thousands of feet above the land below, thereby forming a valley-shaped plateau surface.

Plains

Mexico has very little low-lying flat land. The largest plain is the Yucatán Peninsula. This flat to gently rolling area is a limestone platform that rises above the surrounding Gulf of Mexico and the Caribbean Sea. Water sinks into porous limestone rock and, as it does, rock is dissolved. As a result, the peninsula's surface has no lakes and few streams. Underground, however, erosion has formed caverns. When the roof of a cavern collapses, a sink-hole is formed. These steep-sided features, called cenotes, dot the landscape of Yucatán. Cenotes can reach a depth of nearly 100 feet (35 m). People of the Mayan civilization depended on water contained in the bottom of cenotes for their primary supply of this essential resource.

Narrow coastal plains border both the Atlantic and Pacific coasts. The coastal plain bordering the Gulf of Mexico is flat and lacks major indentations. There are few good natu-ral harbors along this coast. Water is shallow, and there are many sandy offshore islands and sandbars that shelter coastal lagoons. On the mainland, swamps and marshes border much of the low-lying coast. Farther inland, rich soils formed from alluvium (stream-deposited silt) washed down from the Sierra Madre Oriental support much of Mexico's productive plantation agriculture. The west coast is much more rug-ged. Scattered basins separated by mountains dot the coast. In many places, however, mountains plunge steeply into the Pacific Ocean. Many bays, such as those at Acapulco and Puerto Vallarta, form excellent natural harbors and scenic tourist attractions.

WEATHER, CLIMATE, AND ECOSYSTEMS

In many places, weather and climate combine to be the single most important element of the natural environment. It is the primary agent influencing natural vegetation, wildlife habitat, and water features. It is also extremely important to people, often playing a major role in where people live and what they are able (or unable) to do. Most people are concerned with two elements of weather that are of greatest importance to their daily lives: temperature and precipitation. Storms are also of great importance.

Temperature

Northern Mexico's desert region experiences some of the world's hottest temperatures. And most of southern Mexico experiences hot, steamy weather. Yet huge areas of Mexico are cool, and glaciers cling to the northern slope of Mount Orizaba. Several important controls of climate explain these huge differences.

The Tropic of Cancer (23.5 degrees north latitude) runs through central Mexico. The country's latitude—its position on the globe relative to the equator and poles—gives the country a tropical to subtropical climate. But unlike many tropical countries, much of Mexico is cool. This is explained by a second major control of weather: elevation. Anyone who has ever lived or traveled in a mountainous area knows that temperatures drop with increased elevation.

Temperature conditions in Mexico fall into three general categories. First, there is the desert north. Here, summer temperatures can climb to more than 120°F (49°C). In the dry climate, however, there is no blanket of clouds to hold heat near the earth. After sunset, temperatures can drop 50° to 60°F (10° to 16°C) from the day's high. During the winter, *nortes*—cool air masses from the north—move south from Canada and the United States, occasionally bringing freezing weather. Much of coastal, southern, and eastern Mexico does not experience the extremely high temperatures of the desert. But because of higher humidity, temperatures often feel hot and sticky, and nighttime temperatures are warmer. These locations have a higher annual average temperature than the desert. Finally, there are the highlands. Here temperature varies with elevation. A drop of about 3.5°F (1°C) occurs with each 1,000-foot (305-m) increase in elevation. This explains why nights can be so cold in much of Mexico and why glaciers occur on the upper slopes of towering Mount Orizaba.

Mexico's unique weather patterns are highlighted by an event that occurred during late July 1999. It certainly must

Most of Mexico's people live in mountainous areas. In order to find land on which to raise crops to feed the country's rapidly growing population, Mexican farmers have been forced to plant on steep mountain slopes. Erosion takes a heavy toll on exposed mountain soils.

rank as one of the most unusual weather occurrences ever experienced. According to a news report appearing in the Mexico City newspaper *El Universal*:

> More than 20 people were killed in [a] cold snap ... which disrupted transportation across the country. [The] weather system brought almost 16 inches [41 centimeters]

of snow to the southwestern city of Guadalajara, its first snowfall since 1881. Strong winds and rain hit the eastern side of the country . . . where wind speeds reached as high as 75 miles per hour [120 km]. . . . In the central Mexican state of Hidalgo temperatures dropped as low as five degrees below zero [-21°C].

Precipitation

Precipitation is any form of falling moisture. Most precipitation in Mexico falls as rain. But snow does fall during winter months in the north and during much of the year in higher mountainous regions. Hail occasionally accompanies strong thunderstorms, particularly in northern Mexico. Rainfall in much of the country can best be described as being either too little or too much. The northern desert region gets little precipitation during a normal year, with most places receiving only 2 to 10 inches (5 to 25 centimeters). Batagues, a small community near the Colorado River delta, is the driest place in North America. It averages a scant 1 inch (2.5 cm) of rainfall a year and on occasion has gone several years without receiving a drop of rain. In the tropical south, on the other hand, some places receive as much as 200 inches (508 cm) of rain annually.

In locations other than those that are either wet or dry all year, precipitation depends on the season. In fact, seasons in tropical Mexico are based on rainfall, not temperature. "Winter" is the dry season, and "summer" is the wet season. During the winter season, streams and wells often run dry, and crops can wilt as parched soils turn to powder. Rains can be torrential, however, during the summer and early fall. During this time of year, much of the rain falls during tropical storms that move onto land from the Gulf of Mexico or Caribbean Sea.

Tropical Storms

Tropical storms strike both the Atlantic and Pacific coasts of Mexico. Storms in the Caribbean Sea and Gulf of Mexico are the most damaging. These tropical killers usually occur from July through October. A tropical storm becomes a hurricane when winds blow more than 74 miles (119 km) per hour. Such storms can cause terrible destruction of property and human life. In addition to normal wind damage, along low-lying coasts, huge wind-driven waves can destroy everything in their path. Inland, torrential rains that accompany tropical storms can cause severe flooding.

Tropical storms striking the Pacific coast of Mexico usually are less severe. Those that begin over the Pacific's tropical waters and reach the coast of Mexico are called hurricanes. If the storm continues westward over the Pacific, it is called a typhoon. The storms are the same; only the name is different, based on their location.

Mexico's most damaging tropical storm in 40 years struck in early October 1999. A huge storm system stalled for a full week in the Gulf of Mexico, off the coast of southern Mexico. Some coastal towns received a normal year's rainfall in just three days. Inland, torrents of rain loosened mountainsides, causing thundering mudslides that destroyed entire villages. Lowlands turned into raging torrents, creating vast lakes. By the time the storm was over, nearly 250,000 people were homeless and as many as 500 had died. Damage to property, roads and bridges, and crops rose to several billion dollars.

In October 2007, another devastating tropical storm swept into southern Mexico. Nearly all of the southern state of Tabasco was flooded by torrential rains. When the storm subsided, some half million people were homeless in what was one of Mexico's worst natural disasters.

Climate and Vegetation

Most of northern Mexico is arid or semiarid. Summers are very hot, but winters are pleasantly cool. Little precipitation falls during any month. Hardy desert plant life is small and scattered. Both plants and animals of this climate have developed unique means of surviving in the harsh desert environment.

Much of southern and eastern Mexico is humid tropical or subtropical. Temperatures are always warm in the lowlands, and frost never occurs. Most rain falls from May through October. Lowland areas support dense rain forests and savannas, areas of tall grasses with scattered trees.

Because of its tropical and subtropical location, Mexico's climate is greatly influenced by elevation. Geographers identify four vertical zones within tropical areas, each with its own characteristic climate, vegetation, and potential land use.

Elevation	Climate
Above 13,000 ft.	*Tierra helada*—cold or snow covered year-round
5,000–13,000 ft.	*Tierra fria*—cool to cold for all but hardy crops
2,000–5,000 ft.	*Tierra templada*—temperate land, temperate-zone crops
Sea level–2,000 ft.	*Tierra caliente*—hot, wet, tropical lowlands, tropical crops

Tierra caliente (hot land) generally lies at an elevation between sea level and 2,000 feet (610 m). There is little seasonal change in temperatures. Here, it is said that "nighttime is the winter of the tropics" (nighttime temperatures are often colder than average temperatures during the winter months). Frost is unknown. Lush tropical forests and savanna grasslands thrive in this climate. So do tropical crops such as cacao (used in making chocolate), bananas, sugarcane, tobacco, and coconut palms.

Tierra templada (temperate land) is sandwiched between the hot and the cold elevations. Lying between about 2,000 and 5,000 feet (610 and 1,524 m), this climatic zone is a land of eternal spring. Its moderate temperatures and adequate rainfall make this the most desirable area of Mexico. This zone was once home to vast expanses of mixed woodlands. But most of the original plant cover has long been cleared away for farming. Many crops, including corn (maize), potatoes, and the cash crop coffee, thrive here.

Tierra fria (cold land) generally lies between 5,000 and 13,000 feet (1,524 and 3,962 m). Days are usually pleasant, with cool to warm temperatures, depending upon elevation. Nights, however, can be cool to cold. Killing frosts can occur, as can occasional snowfall. A variety of midlatitude crops, including wheat and corn, thrive here. Surprisingly, perhaps, this is the most densely populated part of Mexico. In the tropics, highlands are cooler, healthier, and less humid than are the hot, steamy lowlands. Therefore, they tend to be attractive areas of settlement.

Tierra helada (frozen land), above 13,000 feet (3,962 m), occurs only on the highest mountain peaks. Here, conditions are too cold for crops or human settlement. At higher reaches of this zone, there are permanent fields of snow and even areas of glacial ice on the "shadowed" northern slopes.

NATURAL RESOURCES

Mexico is rich in natural resources. Precious metals, such as silver and gold, attracted early Spanish conquerors to the area. Copper, lead, zinc, and iron ore have helped Mexico's industrial development. Petroleum has been an important contributor to the country's economy since the early twentieth century. Forests have provided building materials and fuel. About 15 percent of the country has excellent soils. Today, the country's natural beauty—its coasts, mountains, tropics, and desert—attracts millions of tourists.

WILDLIFE

Mexico offers very little that is truly unique in terms of wildlife. Fauna in the northern desert region is similar to that in the adjacent southwestern United States. To the south, tropical life forms predominate. For thousands of years, humans and wildlife have competed for space and survival. The result has been a loss of habitat and of the wildlife dependent upon it. Overhunting also has taken its toll on the region's fauna. Three forms of life, each quite different, do warrant special mention: vampire bats, monarch butterflies, and Pacific whales.

Although vampire bats look quite fierce, people rarely need to worry about their bite and the resulting loss of blood. In the late 1990s, however, vampire bats caused an outbreak of rabies that killed thousands of cattle and other animals in southernmost Mexico. Bats bit several dozen humans, some of whom died as a result of rabies. Many people in the region live in shacks without doors or covered windows. This allows the vampire bats to enter at night, while the inhabitants are asleep. A person can be bitten by a bat and not be aware that it happened. Because of the threat of rabies, many people in Latin America's tropics sleep beneath mosquito netting to keep vampire bats away, as well as insects.

Each November, a small area west of Mexico City receives several hundred million visitors. Some have traveled as much as 2,750 miles (4,425 km) from eastern Canada. But these are not the usual tourists to the country. They are monarch butterflies. For tens of thousands of years, the monarchs have made their annual trip from areas east of the Rocky Mountains in the United States and Canada. No one knows why monarchs are drawn to these tiny patches of fir forest nestled in the mountains of central Mexico. During recent years, the number of butterflies arriving has declined, which worries environmentalists. Some blame it on the weather system known as El Niño and unusually cold, wet weather. Others suggest that loggers in the area are illegally cutting away too many trees. During the winter of 2001–2002, an estimated 250 million butterflies died during a severe rainstorm accompanied by freezing temperatures that struck their winter home. Canadian, American, and Mexican environmental groups are working together in an effort to save the butterflies' winter habitat.

The Pacific coast of Baja California is famous for its marine life. One regular visitor to these crystal-clear waters is the gray whale. Each winter, hundreds of the whales migrate some 5,000 miles (around 8,000 km) from the northern Pacific to Baja's San Ignacio Lagoon. The lagoon is one of UNESCO's 180 natural World Heritage Sites; and it is also one of the last undeveloped whale nurseries on the planet. During recent years, the lagoon has been the site of a major controversy. A large international corporation hoped to place the world's largest salt factory on the lagoon, where salt would be taken from seawater. But the huge saltworks would ruin the last place on Earth where the gray whales can mate, give birth, and nurse their young in a safe environment. When humans interact with the natural environment, there are many options. Some people place value on one element of nature—in this case, whales. Others believe that the easily extracted sea salt is the most important natural resource.

In this case, the whales won. Environmental groups throughout the world protested the proposed plant. In the spring of 2000, the corporation backed down and canceled its plans. Whales will continue to migrate to San Ignacio Lagoon and their numbers will continue to grow.

Tourists climb up a pyramid known as "The Church" at the archaeological ruins of Coba, in the Yucatán Peninsula.

CHAPTER

3

Proud Native Heritage

exico was home to one of the world's great early culture hearths—a center of highly advanced agriculture, architecture, arts, science, government, and religion. Today, the country continues to have a strong imprint of native culture. And Mexico (the name itself being taken from one of the early peoples, the Mexica, or Aztecs) takes great pride in its native heritage. It is necessary to look to the distant past in order to understand Mexico's people and their way of life today.

WHO WERE THE FIRST AMERICANS?

Who were the first people to reach the Americas? Where did they come from? How did they get here? During most of the twentieth century, archaeologists (scientists who study early humans) thought they knew the answers to these questions. Now, they are less sure. In fact, the more scientists learn about early Americans, the less seems to be known for certain.

For nearly a century, it was believed that America's earliest people came from Asia. Their route, according to archaeologists, was by way of the Bering Strait, which served as a land bridge. During the Ice Age, sea level dropped perhaps 350 to 400 feet (107 to 122 m), exposing much of what is now the Bering Strait. This dry land presumably made it possible for big-game hunters to cross from Siberia to Alaska. An ice-free corridor between two huge North American ice sheets left open a pathway southward through what is now Canada. From there, the hunters spread out rapidly through the Americas. The people were members of the Mongoloid race (the primary race of people living in eastern Asia). They presumably arrived some 15,000 to 20,000 years ago.

During recent years, however, these beliefs have been challenged. Some scientists doubt that people could have survived the cold temperatures of a narrow corridor sandwiched between two glaciers. In fact, it is even doubtful that an "ice-free corridor" ever existed. Is it possible that the early migrants could have followed a much warmer coastal route on land and along the glaciers' edge by water? Some scientists now believe that the first Americans followed such a route. Recent archaeological finds also suggest that people native to Europe and Africa were in the Americas at very early dates. Might at least a few early Americans have crossed the Atlantic Ocean? Some evidence suggests this might have happened. There is mounting evidence that early humans reached the southern part of South America more than 30,000 years ago. That is nearly twice as long as previous evidence supporting a human presence in North America had shown. And it is much older than any early dates from far northern North America. Who the first Americans were, where they came from, when they arrived, and how they traveled are questions that remain open to doubt.

This much is known about Mexico's early people. First, they were not one group. Their languages, physical appearance, and other evidence suggest that several different groups settled the area. Whether they all came from eastern Asia, or elsewhere, is unknown. Second, they were skilled at living off the land. Some were hunters of big game. The area teemed with large animals. Spear points have been found in the bones of mammoths and other big-game animals long extinct. When humans first arrived, ancestors of the bison (a type of buffalo that roamed the North American plains by the millions), horse, and llama also inhabited the land. Other groups gathered roots, seeds, nuts, and berries. Mexico's tropical location made it possible to find food all year. For thousands of years, the people hunted and gathered, and some living near water fished. The population was low, and people lived in small, widely scattered groups. Most people were nomadic, wandering from place to place in search of food.

In the tropics, the coconut palm satisfied many needs. From the coconut fruit came a refreshing liquid, as well as "meat" and fiber. Wood from its trunk was used for building. Fronds (palm leaves) had many uses, including roofing, wall siding, floor covering, sleeping mats, and baskets. Early native peoples of eastern Mexico chewed an extract of the sapodilla tree. The extract, called chicle, is still enjoyed today by millions of people. Chicle, with flavor added, is better known as chewing gum.

Various kinds of worms and insects provided essential protein to the diet. A favorite even today is the maguey worm. Some people specialize in harvesting the worms, which must be cut carefully from the maguey plant in which they live. When fried, the larvae turn golden brown and crunchy. The list of insects eaten in traditional Mexico is long. Other game that played an important role in the diet of rural people includes iguana lizards, salamanders, and rattlesnakes; and from tropical southern rain forests came caimans (an alligator-like reptile), monkeys, armadillos, and many kinds of rodents that have been prized foods for thousands of years. Of course, you will not find any of these once-favored delicacies in your favorite "Mexican" restaurant! Through time, tastes have changed.

EARLY FARMERS

Many scientists believe that the dawn of agriculture was one of the most important forward leaps in human history. Rather than depending upon hunting and gathering, some people began deliberately to plant and harvest crops and keep animals. They became food producers, and as such they gained much more control over nature and their ability to survive.

When, where, and how farming began in Mesoamerica (the term archaeologists use when referring to the region inhabited by native Middle American civilizations) is not known. What is known is that farming began in only a few places throughout the world. One of them was Mexico. Productive farming provided the foundation upon which all early civilizations were built. This was true of Mexico as well. Some people there began deliberately to plant crops at least 5,000 years ago. It was about that time that a major change began to occur among the region's people.

Archaeologists point to the early stirrings of civilization in the region about 3000 B.C. Some people living in the tropical lowlands and nearby hills bordering the Gulf of Campeche began farming and living in villages. By 1500 B.C., many people living in central and eastern Mexico had also given up hunting, fishing, and gathering to become farmers. By farming, they were able to produce a more reliable and abundant food supply. With ample food, more people could live in one place. Many people began to live much longer. Populations exploded, and villages began to grow both in number and size. Not everyone needed to work the fields. Some people became skilled artisans and craftspeople, while others became priests and healers. There were now specialists, people who knew how to do specific things that village life made both possible and increasingly necessary. Mexico was on the brink of becoming one of the world's great centers of advanced culture and civilization.

Many crops that are essential to today's diet came from Mesoamerica. They include maize (corn), several varieties of beans, squashes, sweet and hot peppers, grain amaranth, tomatoes, and avocados. Other products, contributing to some of today's favorite desserts, are vanilla, chocolate, and papaya.

A MEXICAN CROP TRINITY

The crop "trinity" of maize, beans, and squash has been the foundation of Mexican agriculture for several thousand years. These crops, with the addition of chilis, form the basis of the native Mexican (Indian) diet. They thrive in most Mexican environments and can grow successfully under quite difficult conditions.

Corn is the most important food in Indian Mexico. It is eaten in many different forms. Kernels are toasted, ground into a meal, and eaten either dry or as a porridge. Most people prefer to eat corn as tortillas (round, flat cakes). Tortillas can be eaten alone or used as a wrap to hold meat, beans, and chili. Corn is rich in sugar and provides as much as three-fourths of the daily energy intake in a traditional Mexican diet.

Beans are rich in protein and fat content. Before Europeans introduced domestic livestock, boiled beans were the most important source of essential protein for many Mesoamericans. Squashes and their close relative, pumpkins, are among the oldest crops. They were first planted for their protein-bearing seeds, but their flesh, flowers, and leaves were also eaten.

When one thinks of "Mexican food," almost certainly "hot" (spicy) is the first thing that comes to mind. Many varieties of chili peppers thrive in the region. Some are eaten raw; others are used to make salsa or other kinds of sauces. Chilis are a source of essential vitamins and also aid in digestion. Together, corn, beans, squash, and chili peppers form a nutritious and well-balanced diet.

Corn is an important crop and is used as a staple ingredient in Mexican food. For example, tortillas made of ground corn are used as bread at many meals.

RISE OF CIVILIZATION

Central and eastern Mexico were home to one of the world's great centers of early civilization. As farming improved, harvests were greater and food surpluses were larger. Specialization increased. Pots, jewelry, and other items were no longer made only for home use; they also began being made as trade items. Cities grew, with some becoming important market and trading centers. Others became ceremonial centers, with burial mounds, pyramids, and temples.

Many cultures contributed to the rise of civilization in Mexico. Over a period of some 3,000 years, the center of highest culture shifted from place to place. Civilization first emerged on the low-lying coastal plain bordering the Gulf of Mexico, then it flourished on the Yucatán Peninsula, and finally it developed on the high Central Plateau. Through time, the native cultures responsible for great achievements and works also changed. Chief among them were the lowland Olmec and Mayans. In the interior highlands, the unknown builders of the giant city Teotihuacán, and later the Aztec (Mexica) people, rose to great power.

OLMEC (1500 B.C.–A.D. 200)

The Olmec occupied forested coastal lowlands of the present-day states of Veracruz and Tabasco. In the beginning, they farmed corn, but they also hunted and fished. However, they learned to put to good use several things found within their natural environment: trees that produced cacao and rubber (the name *Olmec* means "Rubber People"); salt extracted from the nearby Gulf of Mexico; and a kind of stone that was used to make *manos* and *metates* (tools used to grind corn into meal). These items were the basis of lively trade that linked Olmec centers with communities throughout much of Mesoamerica.

The Olmec were creative. They were one of the earliest people in the Americas to make pottery. And they were one of the first people to develop a simple written form of communication. The Olmec also built the first pyramids in the Americas—structures as large or larger in mass than those of Egypt. Their large buildings were made with beautifully carved stone. They were skillful painters and sculptors and also made beautiful jewelry from jade (obtained in trade from Guatemala) and other stones.

These ancient people are best known for one of the great mysteries of American archaeology—the many huge stone heads that they left behind. The heads measure up to nine feet (2.74 m) in height and weigh as much as 10 tons (9 metric tons). Some scientists say they look "foreign," and have suggested they look African because of their broad noses; others believe they look Asian because of their eyes. Still others suggest that they are monuments to honor Olmec leaders who died. Because all of the heads have what appears to be a helmet of some kind, it has even been suggested that they were created to honor ballplayers who became heroes for winning a game.

The Olmec left other things, as well. Who does not love a delicious chocolate bar, chocolate cake or ice cream, or a cup of hot chocolate on a cold winter evening? Chocolate, made from the beans of the cacao tree, originally came from Mexico. It is believed that the Olmec were the first to domesticate the cacao tree and to discover the use of chocolate as a drink. Chocolate in ancient Mexico was different than the sweet chocolate enjoyed today. Natives used it to make a drink that was dark and bitter, and they drank it cold. It was not until after the Spaniards arrived, bringing sugarcane, that sugar was added and chocolate began to taste sweet.

History shows that New World peoples did not use the wheel for transportation. This important invention—one of the most important ever—first appeared in southwestern Asia, perhaps 6,000 years ago. It was used on carts and later on chariots to carry warriors into battle. The Olmec had the idea of the wheel, but they used it only to make toys. Several small animal-like toys mounted on wheels have been found. In Mexico, the wheel was used for play, rather than for work. Why was the wheel, one of humankind's most useful tools, not used for work among the Indians of Mesoamerica? (They did not have large domesticated animals or the idea of a harness to link a power source with something pulled.) How might the cultures of Middle America been different had they used the wheel for work?

It is not known why the Olmec culture died out. Perhaps their homeland was struck by some devastating environmental disaster, such as a hurricane or severe drought. Some archaeologists believe that disease may have destroyed the population or weakened the social structure. There are many theories, but no one really knows. The huge stone heads that have survived relatively unharmed over the centuries are all that provide a glimpse of these ancient peoples.

MAYANS (1100 B.C.–A.D. 900)

The Mayan civilization began in the areas that are now Guatemala and Belize and gradually spread into the Yucatán Peninsula. These creative people became Mesoamerica's most advanced native culture. The Mayans built dozens of cities and ceremonial centers. Huge plazas, pyramids, and buildings were built of stone without the use of metal tools. Many well-preserved Mayan ruins dot the landscape of southeastern Mexico today. These ruins reveal a great deal about Mayan culture.

Some ruins suggest that the Mayans were skilled in making accurate astronomical observations. It is known that they were skilled in mathematics. They used the zero, an idea that at the time was understood by only two other cultures, Babylonians and Hindus. Using astronomy and mathematics, they were able to make a calendar that is more accurate than the one we use today. The Mayans were also the first people in the Americas to have a well-developed written language. Writing made it possible for them to record their history, keep track of time, and note important religious ideas and events.

Sometime during the ninth century A.D., a catastrophe struck the Mayans. Cities throughout the region were abandoned, and their civilization vanished. Many scientists have tried to explain the Mayan decline. Some suggest drought, land erosion, or disease; others believe that warfare, social disorder, or overpopulation might have been the cause. But no one really knows what brought about the end of what at the time was North America's most advanced culture. Millions of Mayan-speaking people continue to live in the region today. It was the civilization that disappeared, not the Mayan people themselves.

TEOTIHUACÁN (CA. A.D. 200 TO
LAST HALF OF SEVENTH CENTURY A.D.)

One of the greatest mysteries in New World archaeology rises above the valley floor about 30 miles (48.2 km) northeast of Mexico City. Here are the ruins of Teotihuacán (Place of the Gods), once the largest city in the Americas and perhaps in the world at the time. An estimated 125,000 to 200,000 people lived peacefully in the shadow of two huge pyramids. The 180-foot-high (55-meter-high) Pyramid of the Sun is the world's largest, being greater at its base than even the largest Egyptian pyramid.

Teotihuacán was a ceremonial center believed to have begun around A.D. 200. It grew to become a major center of manufacturing and trade. Archaeologists believe that up to 25 percent of the city's people were involved in the production of crafts. The most popular crafts were items made from obsidian (volcanic glass—a gift from the nearby mountains). Teotihuacán was also located on major trade routes. Goods made in the city have been found all over Mesoamerica.

But many mysteries surround the city. No one knows what group of people built Teotihuacán. Little is known of their

Teotihuacán remains one of the world's greatest archaeological mysteries. Nearly 2,000 years ago, a people whose language and cultural identity is unknown created what became the most populated city in the Americas and one of the largest in the world. Towering over the huge urban trade center was the Pyramid of the Sun, which in mass and base dimensions is the world's largest pyramidal structure.

government. Neither tombs of rulers nor statues of leaders have been found. How and why did they build huge pyramids? In an area known for conflict, how were they able to live in peace? No fortifications have been discovered, and there is no evidence of soldiers or war. What language did they speak? The greatest mystery, however, is why the city withered and died sometime late in the seventh century A.D.

Teeth and bones of these ancient people provide clues, and what they reveal is important for cities today. Archaeologists believe that during the seventh century, the city experienced urban decay—pollution and disease were killing many residents. Teeth and bones show evidence of poor nutrition, infections, and disease.

What happened to cause these conditions? It seems likely that pollution and poor sanitation caused the problems. It is also possible that the city grew so large that it was unable to feed its population. Once again, the importance of wise human interaction with the environment is clear. Within 50 years, the largest city in the Americas, and one of the largest in the world, became a ghost town.

AZTECS (LATE TWELFTH CENTURY–1520s)

For several thousand years, civilization had flourished on the tropical lowlands of southeastern Mexico. The country's dry north was home to small bands of Chichimec, a name given collectively to many tribes that roamed the region. They had few possessions, were few in number, and left few landmarks. However, one of these groups, the Mexica, soon changed Mexico's history forever. The Mexica, later known as Aztecs, were to build a great city and become rulers of the land that today bears their name: Mexico. By the end of the twelfth century, the Olmec and Mayan civilizations had long disappeared, as had the people of Teotihuacán. It was in this cultural setting that the Mexica wandered southward and entered the Valley of Mexico. On an island in large Lake Texcoco, they found refuge from hostile groups living in and around the valley. In 1325, they began building a city they called Tenochtitlán.

By 1430, the Aztecs had learned many important things. They learned farming from neighboring tribes in the valley.

They had also become a major military power. Soon, using threats and force, they began spreading their control throughout the region. By 1500, they had carved out the biggest empire Mesoamerica had ever known. Some 30 million people were under their rule (at the time, the most populated country in Europe had only about 20 million people). It was governed from Tenochtitlán, which had become a huge and magnificent city.

Building the Aztec capital was difficult. Mud from the bottom of Lake Texcoco was dredged to build the city's foundations. New land was made for farming by building islands in the shallow lake. These islands, called *chinampas*, became the world's most productive farmland. Causeways and bridges were built to link the city with the lakeshore. Within the city, people traveled on tree-lined canals.

Conquered people were forced to pay tribute to the Aztecs. From all over the empire came food, woven goods, tropical products, feathers, gold, and other precious items. Tribute often included human prisoners. These unfortunate people, as well as prisoners taken in battle by the Aztecs, faced a terrible fate—they were sacrificed to the Aztec gods. The Aztecs believed that their gods had sacrificed themselves for mankind and that their blood had given humans life. Human life, the Aztecs believed, was the best gift they could give their gods to keep them content.

The Aztecs practiced human sacrifice on a huge scale, reportedly killing as many as 20,000 captured prisoners in one day in 1487. Victims were taken to the top of a temple or pyramid and placed upon an altar. While priests held their arms and legs, another priest, using a razor-sharp obsidian knife (made of volcanic glass), plunged the blade into the victim's chest, ripping it open. The still beating heart was torn from the body, held high in offering to the gods, and then burned. The body was pushed down the steep steps and another victim was brought to the altar. This inhumane practice continued for more than a century.

The Aztecs had two calendars, one for the solar year and another for the religious ritual year. The solar-year calendar had 365 days (as does ours), and the ritual calendar had a year lasting 260 days. The two calendars "met" every 52 years. According to Aztec beliefs, after 52 years the world would end unless appropriate action was taken. This period was the most important in Aztec religious life; it also was believed to be the most dangerous period in human life. During this time, there were many religious rituals, including increased human sacrifice.

Writing was used for many purposes, including keeping diaries and noting historical events. This is why more is known about Aztec history than about any other early Native American peoples. Aztec boys and girls attended school, where they learned about their history, religion, and myths. They also learned songs, poems, and how to behave. Boys were taught about agriculture and various other trades and skills. They also received military training.

By 1520, the Aztecs had gained many enemies. Their neighbors were tired of paying tribute. And they were tired of having their people sacrificed to please the Aztec gods. Change was in the air, and things seemed to be falling apart. Little could the Aztecs, or other native cultures in the region, imagine what was about to happen.

According to an Aztec myth, a light-skinned priest-king named Quetzalcoátl had once arrived from a distant homeland far across the sea. Quetzalcoátl was against human sacrifices, and this made him unpopular with some Aztec rulers. In disgust, according to legend, Quetzalcoátl set sail eastward from the coast of Veracruz aboard a raft made of snakes. He promised someday to return from the east in the year One Reed—the one that falls once every 52 years in the Aztec calendar. This is the year of dread, the year of disaster, the year they believed the world could end. In that year, a Spanish adventurer named Hernán Cortés set sail for Mexico. In many ways, the myth of Quetzalcoátl was about to come true.

The Spaniards, under the leadership of explorer Hernán Cortés, fought the Aztecs for two years. Although heavily outnumbered, they were finally victorious, conquering the city of Tenochtitlán after a fierce battle in August 1521.

4

Spanish Conquest

The imprint of Mexico's native heritage is deeply embedded in the country's distinctive landscapes and the way of life of its people. But so is the imprint of a people and culture from a far distant land—Spain. Five centuries ago, with the arrival of Spanish conquerors, a massive change began to take place in Mexico. This chapter discusses the sixteenth-century Spanish conquest. In many ways, this is the most important period in Mexico's history. The imprint of this event is evident in all aspects of Mexican landscapes and life. Spanish influence spread during the colonial period through the area that is now Mexico (and far beyond). Finally, it is important to understand how Spanish influence shaped Mexico's present-day land, people, and way of life.

As is often the case when cultures collide, the outcome can be catastrophic. When studying the Spanish conquest and its results, it is important to recognize the terrible impact this event had on the native peoples. For many, it brought death. For those still living, it was a shocking and often tragic time of great hardship and shattering change.

A CATACLYSMIC COLLISION OF CULTURES

In April 1519, a young Spanish adventurer—Hernán Cortés—landed on the coast of what is now the state of Veracruz. He had a navy of 11 ships and 100 sailors. He also brought 508 soldiers, 16 horses, and 14 cannons. Spaniards, who had arrived in the Caribbean 27 years earlier, had heard tales of a golden city someplace in Mexico. Cortés was in search of this wealth. Little did he know that perhaps 15 to 20 million people—and one of the world's great civilizations—occupied the lands beyond the horizon.

In 1519, Montezuma II ruled the huge and powerful Aztec empire. The Aztecs were at the peak of their power, but how could anyone guess what was about to happen? Montezuma was very superstitious. He believed the legend of Quetzal-coátl—the tale of a bearded white god who promised to return one day and destroy the Aztec empire. Imagine Montezuma's shock when messengers arrived telling him that hundreds of bearded white men had arrived on the coast. And that they had arrived on April 22, the date on which, according to the legend, Quetzalcoátl was supposed to return.

In panic, Montezuma sent the god (who was actually Cortés) many presents in the hope that he would not destroy his empire. Among the gifts were a number of gold ornaments. Cortés, lured by reports of a golden city, believed he had found what he was searching for. His soldiers, however, had heard other stories—about fierce Aztec warriors. Many wanted to return to the Caribbean islands. Afraid that he might lose his men, Cortés burned all his ships before heading inland. Now there could be no turning back.

The weather was hot and humid, which made the march inland difficult. The Sierra Madre Oriental rose as a huge wall to be climbed via steep and often treacherous trails. And seemingly at every turn, Indian warriors attacked the Spaniards. The Indians, however, were no match for the Spaniards, who had armor, horses, guns, and ferocious fighting dogs.

On the way to the Aztec capital of Tenochtitlán, Cortés had some amazing good fortune. He met an Indian woman who spoke many languages of the region. The woman, named Doña Marina by the Spaniards, could translate for Cortés. He was able to explain his plan to Indians representing different tribes along the route. Many of these tribal peoples hated their ruthless Aztec rulers. They gladly threw their support to the Spaniards when they learned that Cortés planned to conquer their enemy.

It took the Spaniards three months to travel about 180 miles (290 km) from the coast to the Valley of Mexico. When the Spaniards got their first glimpse of the huge valley, its many lakes, and the magnificent capital city of Tenochtitlán, it must have been one of the great moments of history. Spread out before them was one of the world's most beautiful vistas. Imagine their shock as they gazed upon a civilization that rivaled any existing in Europe at the time. It is little wonder that they cried out, "It is the promised land!"

FALL OF THE AZTEC EMPIRE

Two years passed before Cortés and his soldiers finally conquered the fierce Aztecs. Tenochtitlán fell on August 21, 1521. The city was in ruins, and the proud Aztec empire was destroyed with it. Many things worked together to make the conquest possible.

First, the Spaniards had superior military capability. Their armor protected them from arrows. The Aztecs had never before seen horses. In fact, they believed that horse and man were one—like the huge, ferocious centaur of Greek mythology.

The Spaniards also had guns, cannons, and fierce fighting dogs capable of tearing a human to shreds. Second, the Aztecs were cruel rulers who were hated by their neighbors. Many tribes joined the Spaniards in their fight against the Aztecs. Third, the Spaniards were able to surround the island city of Tenochtitlán and block access to its onshore food supply. Finally, millions of Indians began to die from diseases introduced by the Europeans. Historians often write about the bravery and skill of Spanish soldiers. It is important to remember that they had a great deal of help, including from native peoples, as well as what for them was simply good luck.

A TIME OF GREAT CHANGE

With the conquest came great change. The Spaniards immediately began to place their imprint on the Mexican people and landscape. For the native peoples, the results were disastrous.

During the long siege, Tenochtitlán was completely destroyed by the Spaniards. Much of the damage was done in battle, but after the war was over, Spaniards destroyed everything that remained standing. They did not want the Aztecs to have reminders of their religion or empire, or any other link to their past. From the ruins of Tenochtitlán would rise a new magnificent capital—the Spanish-built Ciudad de Mexico (Mexico City).

The new Spanish city was different in many ways. Rather than teeming with Native Americans, it was now home to people of a strange culture from a land far across the sea. Gone were the Aztec ceremonial centers and homes. In their place appeared Catholic churches and Spanish-style homes. A new language was heard in its streets, as Spanish replaced the Aztec's Nahuatl tongue. New crops appeared in fields, new and strange foods appeared on dining tables, and previously unknown animals began grazing the countryside. With the Aztec empire gone, Spain would rule over Nueva España (New Spain, the name by which Mexico was then known) for the next 300 years. The area surrounding

Tenochtitlán may have had a population of nearly 500,000 at the time of conquest. It was the largest city in the Americas, and possibly in the world. Five hundred years later, Mexico City is once again the largest urban center in the Americas and one of the largest in the world. What makes this fact so amazing is that it is also the world's largest city at the highest elevation and the world's only national capital not located on a river.

INDIAN POPULATIONS

With the arrival of the Spaniards, two things happened to the Indian populations: a drastic decrease in numbers and widespread racial intermixing. It is difficult to know how many people lived in Mexico when the Spaniards arrived. Estimates range from under 10 million to as many as 25 million. What is known is that within 100 years of the conquest, only about 1.2 million remained. In many Spanish-settled areas, Indian people disappeared completely.

A number of things combined to cause this huge drop in the Indian population. Many people died in the fighting that accompanied the conquest. Some were taken as slaves and died while captive. Many families simply did not want to have children. They did not want to bring youngsters into a world in which they would suffer under Spanish rule. The primary cause of population decline, however, was disease. Native Americans were not immune to Old World illnesses such as mumps, measles, and smallpox. Flu, malaria, and even the common cold were also new to the Indians. Millions of people died from these and other introduced illnesses. Today, there are few pure Indians or Spaniards in Mexico. Centuries of intermarriage between Indian and European peoples created a new "race," called mestizos.

SPANISH CULTURAL IMPRINT

With the conquest and resulting death of millions of native peoples, Spanish culture began to replace native ways of living.

The Indians rapidly and willingly accepted some Spanish things, such as new crops and animals. Others, such as Roman Catholicism and patterns of settlement, were forced upon the native peoples. Still others, including the Spanish language and system of government, were accepted very slowly.

Many native languages were spoken in preconquest Mexico. Today, native tongues can still be heard in some remote areas of the country. Mayan, for example, is still spoken throughout the Yucatán Peninsula. And the Aztec language, Nahuatl, can still be heard in many villages in the mountains of east-central Mexico. Language change is usually based on need. If a person can benefit in some way from learning a new language, he or she will learn it. Most Indians living among Spaniards learned Spanish. So did those native peoples who were involved in Spanish economic activities. Many people, even today, speak both their native tongue and Spanish.

Roman Catholic priests came to Mexico with the conquerors. Their goal was to convert the Indians to Catholicism. Within 200 years, nearly the entire population of the country was Catholic. Conversion, however, simply meant being baptized in the faith. The Indians often had no idea what this strange ritual meant, or, in fact, that they were now supposedly Catholic. Even today, in remote areas of Mexico, Catholic services are often a blend of Roman, Spanish, and native traditions.

In time, the Roman Catholic Church became the most powerful force in Mexico. Each community had at least one church, and larger communities had many. According to historians, nearly 12,000 churches were built during the era of Spanish rule. Many of these buildings stand today. Their size and beauty are reminders of the power and importance of the church during the colonial era.

The Catholic clergy did more than build churches and try to save souls. They built hospitals and schools. In fact, the oldest university in the Americas was started in 1551; it was built

In the Spanish tradition, important public buildings were placed adjacent to the public square. The Cathedral of Mexico City (left) and the National Palace (right) face the Plaza de la Constitucion, one of the world's largest public squares, located in the nation's capital.

and run by the Catholic Church. Priests and nuns were teachers, doctors, nurses, artists, and writers. They built villages, introduced new types of architecture, and brought new crops and farming techniques.

Where people lived and the layout of their communities also changed under Spanish rule. Spaniards had a long tradition of living in towns and cities. Under their rule, many new communities appeared. One of the most important types of

Spanish settlement was the *villa* (town). These villages were small and compact. Larger communities were called *ciudad* (city). Even today, many Mexican communities include "Villa" or "Ciudad" as part of their name.

Communities, regardless of their size, were carefully laid out in a checkerboard-like grid pattern. At the heart of each villa or ciudad was the town plaza or square. The church, public buildings, important businesses, and homes of wealthy or socially important people faced the plaza. The plaza was the town's economic and social center. Colorful markets were regularly held in its open space. At night, it became a social gathering place that was alive with sounds of people and music.

Spaniards built many new communities so they could better control the Indians. Before the conquest, most Indians lived in small, widely scattered villages. The government wanted them in compact towns. When gathered together, it was easier for the Spaniards to collect tribute and to use the Indians for labor. The Catholic Church also built villages. With Indians living together in a community, it was easier for a priest to keep them under his watchful eye. Sometimes, the forced resettlement of Indians had severe results. Some locations were poorly suited to farming, so food production dropped and many people starved. Also, so many people living close together encouraged the spread of diseases, resulting in many deaths. But these small farming villages, built around a central plaza and church, became a major feature of Mexico's landscape.

The Spaniards also introduced their own preferred building styles. To anyone traveling in Mexico today, the many old buildings in each community serve as an obvious reminder of the country's Spanish colonial past. Towering churches, stately public buildings, and centuries-old homes add both interest and beauty to the region's cultural landscape.

During the Spanish colonial period, no building could rise higher than the church. This rule meant that throughout

Mexico, the church was (and often continues to be) the most prominent building in every community. Indians working under the direction of priests built most of the churches. Many larger towns served as church administrative centers. Convents, cathedrals, and other church-related structures added to the importance of the religious imprint on the landscape.

Before the Spaniards arrived, the mountain slopes of central Mexico were covered with dense forests of oak, pine, and fir. Indians had used stone and small amounts of wood for much of their building. But the Spanish used large amounts of wood in building their villas and churches. Spaniards also used charcoal (made from wood) for heating and cooking. Indians soon learned this practice as well. Because of overcutting, forests began to disappear around villages. Within a century, very few trees remained on the mountain slopes of central Mexico. Erosion became a serious problem, creating huge scars on slopes that once were densely wooded. Silt washed down from the mountainsides and began choking the many lakes that dotted the floor of the Valley of Mexico. Today, charcoal is still widely used, and the few remaining areas of woodland are fast disappearing.

EARLY COLONIAL MEXICO

After the fall of the Aztecs, the Spaniards' stronghold was the Valley of Mexico. Mexico City was built in the heart of the former Aztec empire—it rose from the ruins of Tenochtitlán to become the capital of New Spain. This was the name given by the Spaniards to their newly gained territory in Middle America. From this center of power, the Spaniards launched a conquest of other lands. First, they spread their control southward through Central America. Then, they spread their territory northward into what is now much of the western United States.

Within a decade of the fall of Tenochtitlán, Spaniards had conquered most of the areas of high Indian culture in Mesoamerica. Several factors made this rapid spread of Spanish control possible. Many of the Indians were peaceful farmers who already were accustomed to outside rule. They simply paid tribute to the Spaniards as they previously had done to the Aztecs. Many Indians no doubt thought that it was better to be a slave working for Spaniards than to be a slave offered in sacrifice by Aztec priests. Spaniards held a strong advantage over the Indians with their superior military power. And in many areas, the Indians' will to resist was weakened by the European diseases that were sweeping through New Spain and decimating their populations.

Two important factors helped direct the spread of Spanish control from its core in Mexico City. One factor was the location of dense Indian populations. The other factor was the location of gold.

FORCED INDIAN LABOR

The earliest spread of Spanish culture and control of native land and peoples was into areas with dense Indian populations. After the conquest, the Spanish imposed a harsh system, called *encomienda,* on the conquered Indians. They divided Indian villages among themselves to rule and exploit. Along with the village and use of surrounding land, members of the conquering Spanish force were given control of Indians, who were forced to pay tribute and perform labor. Tribute came in the form of cacao (chocolate), gold, cotton, cloth, and other valuable products that Spaniards could sell for a profit. As laborers, the Indians were forced to work for the Spaniards in fields, in mines, or at other assigned tasks. In return, they were to be taught Spanish and Catholicism. The encomienda system was popular among the Spaniards because it gave them a source of free labor and resulting wealth.

THE LURE OF GOLD AND SILVER

It has been said that the Spaniards came to the New World in search of "glory, God, and gold." Finding gold brought glory, as did the conversion of Indians to the Catholic faith. Throughout the Spanish colonial period in the Americas, however, Spanish settlement and activity most often was associated with mineral wealth—particularly gold. This was true in Mexico as well.

A large belt of gold reached from the Pacific coast near Colima, eastward to the Isthmus of Tehuantepec. One of the richest deposits in this belt is the Valley of Oaxaca. Cortés claimed this land himself. Here, Spaniards used the encomienda system to provide them with Indian labor to work the gold placers (taking gold from streambed gravel). Soon, silver ore was found as well.

The growing and increasingly far-flung Spanish population needed food, fiber, and other agricultural products. Farming of Old World crops, such as wheat, began in cool upland basins. Sugarcane grew well in the hot, wet coastal lowlands and nearby valleys on the flanks of the mountains. The Spaniards introduced Old World livestock into the Americas. Cattle ranches began to thrive in upland grasslands and lowland savannas.

To the south and east, in the Chiapas Highlands and the low-lying limestone peninsula of Yucatán, native peoples put up fierce resistance. No gold was found in either area. And neither the rugged highlands of Chiapas nor the low, infertile limestone plain of Yucatán was suitable for farming. Therefore, neither area attracted many Spaniards. Today, nearly 500 years later, both regions remain strongholds of Native American population and culture.

Northern Mexico presented some problems for the Spanish conquerors. Much of the area was sizzling hot during the long summer and bone dry throughout most of the year. It held little interest for the Spaniards. Also, the north was not settled by "civilized" Indians who could offer the Spaniards valuable tribute. This was home to the fierce, wandering tribes collectively referred to as the Chichimec. These proud people were to be a thorn in the side of the Spaniards (and later Mexicans) for several centuries. Of greatest importance, however,

Taxco is one of many old Spanish colonial silver mining centers. Today, the city attracts thousands of tourists who are interested in learning about the history, colonial architecture, and the shops featuring jewelry and other goods made of silver.

was the absence of known gold deposits. Faced with these obstacles, the northward expansion of New Spain was stopped at the border of this harsh territory the Spaniards called *La Gran Chichimeca—Tierra de Guerra* (the Great [Area] of Chichimecs—Land of War).

Two things happened during the 1540s that opened part of the northern frontier to Spanish settlement. First, the Spanish defeated several hostile Chichimec Indian groups. With the victory, they were able to move the frontier still farther northward. Soon after, in 1546, a second important event occurred. A very rich deposit of silver was discovered in Zacatecas. Thousands of Spaniards poured into the region to seek their fortunes. By the end of the sixteenth century, about 5,000 silver mines were in production. Vast wealth was beginning to flow from Mexico to Spain. In fact, Mexican silver made New Spain the richest of all Spanish colonies worldwide.

Mining, growing wheat, and ranching went hand in hand in colonial Mexico. The reason for this relationship is clear— miners have to eat. Wheat, the favorite grain of Spaniards, was grown in upland areas throughout much of the country. Livestock were also raised throughout much of Mexico to feed hungry miners. Gold was often dredged from stream gravels. In pure form, it could be hand picked and easily carried by a miner. This did not require the use of livestock. Silver, however, was found in combination with other rocks and minerals. Huge quantities of ore had to be moved. Pack animals were needed to mix and haul the ore. Animal fat (tallow) was used to make candles to light dark mine shafts. Animal hide was used to make the sacks and ropes used to hoist the ore to the surface. Mules and horses did the work; cattle and sheep provided food, tallow, leather and, from sheep, wool.

EXPANDING BEYOND THE SILVER FRONTIER

With silver wealth pouring in, rich *reales de minas* (mining camps) grew and prospered. But just beyond the area of silver mining was a northern frontier into which few Spaniards wanted to venture. The desert nomads continued to be a constant threat to further northern expansion. To protect trails and settlers against the Chichimecs, the Spanish built a string of presidios, or forts. Many of the presidios grew to become towns in northern Mexico. Roman Catholic missionaries were also responsible for moving the Spanish settlement frontier northward. Missionaries originally settled many communities in northern Mexico and what is now the southwestern United States.

Spaniards spread their influence northward in other ways as well. In 1540, Francisco de Coronado led an expedition northward into the upper Rio Grande Valley. He was in search of the legendary Seven Cities of Gold that had been reported earlier by another Spaniard, Álvar Núñez Cabeza de Vaca. Spaniards founded Santa Fe (in present-day New Mexico) in 1610, making it the oldest state capital in the United States. At the end of the seventeenth century, Jesuit missionaries had built missions in what is now southern Arizona, claiming that land for New Spain. North of the Rio Grande, San Antonio (in present-day Texas) was settled in 1718, and from there, Spaniards lay claim to much of what is now Texas. Finally, they reached into present-day California. San Diego was settled as a mission in 1769. By the end of the eighteenth century, 21 Catholic missions extended from San Diego to north of the San Francisco Bay. New Spain (and later Mexico) lay claim to the southern half of what is now the United States west of the Rocky Mountains and also part of Texas.

Within 250 years, by the mid-1700s, what is now Mexico had filled in its present territory and reached far beyond. Spanish control over New Spain lasted for three centuries, until 1821, when Mexico gained its independence. The lands Mexico controlled in the southwestern United States eventually were lost. Although Spain was no longer a political factor, Spanish culture had replaced the native ways of living throughout much of the country.

Historians, anthropologists, geographers, and others argue over the cultural impact left by the era of Spanish control. Some point to the "sixteenth century Spanish cultural baggage" under which Mexico and the rest of Latin America continue to struggle even today. Society continues to be highly stratified. Government tends to be unreliable, with power held by a small minority of people who care little about the country or population as a whole. Corruption is widespread and discourages economic development. Wealth tends to be concentrated in the hands of a few and grinding poverty is widespread. Although Mexico has been independent for nearly two centuries, the country still has a long way to go before it overcomes many of the Spanish-introduced traits. Yet the country has benefitted in many ways from the Spanish cultural imprint. One thing is certain: Mexico was forever changed by the clash of civilizations that resulted from the conquest and its aftermath.

Mexico City is the world's third-largest metropolitan center, with an estimated population of approximately 21.2 million. It occupies the site of the former Aztec capital, Tenochtitlán, in the Valley of Mexico. Lake Texcoco was drained during the early seventeenth century, and the Mexican capital rises above the former lake bottom in a setting surrounded on three sides by high mountains, including some active volcanoes.

5

Population and Settlement

Understanding a country's population is an important key to understanding its geography. Is its population large or small? Is the country "overpopulated"? (Does it have too many people for its resources and economy to support?) Are there too few people to develop its land and resources? Where do its people live? Is the population healthy and able to provide for its basic needs? Are many people moving from place to place and, if so, from where to where and why? Answers to questions such as these help shed light on a country's geographic conditions.

There are many ways to study population. Numbers of people are an important factor. So is the density of population and its distribution throughout a region. Trends in population change are also revealing. Of greatest importance, perhaps, is the impact of a country's population on other conditions, such as its economy and the environment.

From this chapter, you will gain a better understanding of the Mexican people—their numbers, where they live, how they live, their differences, and why many of them move.

POPULATION

With approximately 113 million people (2010 estimate), Mexico ranks twelfth among the world's countries in population. And the country's numbers grow by about 1.1 percent, or nearly 1,250,000 people, each year. Many people believe that Mexico's biggest problem is too many people.

If Mexico's present rate of growth continues, the country's population will double in 65 years. The country is relatively poor. It is unable to provide important services—like health care and education—to a booming population. Many people wonder how Mexico will be able to meet the needs of a population expected to reach 200 million by midcentury—well within the lifetime of most readers of this book. Already, more than half the population lacks clean water and safe sanitation facilities. Only about two of every three Mexican youngsters attend school. Many Mexicans cannot find jobs. Even among people who hold jobs, one in every three workers makes wages so low that they are barely able to provide for their family's basic needs. If people's lives are going to improve, the country's economy must grow faster than its population. During recent years, however, population growth has outstripped economic gains. When this happens, most Mexicans become even poorer.

As is true of many poor countries, Mexico has a young population. Nearly 30 percent of the people are under 15 years of age, and only about 6 percent of its population is 65 or older. By comparison, only 20 percent of the U.S. population is under 15, and 13 percent is 65 or older. In Mexico, life expectancy is 76; in the United States it is 78. With a young population and a relatively long life expectancy, the country's population is sure to continue growing at an alarming rate.

At the time of conquest in the early 1500s, Mexico's population is estimated to have been between 10 and 25 million. Within 100 years, the population had dropped to barely 1 million. It was not until 1940—400 years later—that population rebounded to reach its preconquest level. By that time, however, the country's population was exploding. What caused the country's twentieth-century population explosion? By 1950, Mexico's population was one of the world's fastest growing. Today, its annual growth rate of 1.1 percent is well below its record high and comparable to the world average.

Mexico's twentieth-century burst in population growth is easily explained. It is a pattern that has happened repeatedly in economically less developed countries (LDCs) throughout the world. It occurs when modern technology is suddenly introduced into a traditional society. Improved medicine, better hygiene, clean water, and a more reliable food supply combine to allow death rates to drop sharply. Meanwhile, birth rates continue to remain high for some time. More people live beyond their childhood years, and more people live to a much older age. This is the cause of the population explosion.

Fortunately, the unsustainably high rate of population growth during much of the twentieth century has dropped sharply. This, too, is easily explained. More women are going to school, and many women now have jobs. Most men and women do not want to have as many children as did their own parents. Also, in the past, most Mexicans lived in the country. Worldwide, rural families are larger than those living in cities. Today, three of every four Mexican families live in a city, where they want and have fewer children.

FAMILY DECISIONS

Like so many parents in rural Mexican families, Anna Ruiz has trouble remembering the birthdays of her 16 children. "Each one is a blessing from God," Señora Ruiz is quick to say. "Each of them helps the family in so many ways." She carefully explains the chores for which each child is responsible and goes on to say, "Without their help, it would be impossible to survive." Tasks include gathering firewood, carrying water from the village well, and helping with work around the dirt-floored, adobe house. Several youngsters watch over the family's small herd of livestock. Others work in the fields with their father, Manuel. Their needs are few. They are able to grow most of what they need. And each child makes a valuable contribution to the family's well-being.

Hector and Alicia Delgado live in the city. Hector is a professor at the university; Alicia is the manager of a large and successful travel agency. They have one child, a daughter, Marissa. When asked why they do not have more children, Alicia is quick to say, "Small families live much better." Hector adds, "We both love children. But in the city, they are so expensive. Clothes, shoes, backpacks, books . . . it costs hundreds of pesos just to get the things that Marissa needs for school." Alicia goes on to add, "It is so important that we both work. We want to travel, to have a nice home, and be able to send Marissa to college in Europe or the United States."

Both families, of course, are "right." Traditional country people, like the Ruiz family, have few needs for day-to-day living. For them, life is simple: They are able to gather, grow, or make nearly everything they need to live well. All but the very youngest children make important contributions to the family's household needs.

City life, on the other hand, is demanding; urban people have many more needs. Yet urban people are not able to produce the many things they need to live comfortably. By holding jobs, however, they can earn an income. With money, they can buy the food, goods, and services they need. Unlike rural children, only rarely can city kids hold jobs and contribute money to their family. And for city families, each additional child is a new drain on limited family finances.

IS MEXICO "OVERPOPULATED"?

Overpopulation is a difficult idea to define. Some people use crowding to explain overpopulation. But many countries with a high standard of living are extremely crowded. Japan, for example, is six times more densely crowded (people per square mile/kilometer) than Mexico. But Japan's average per capita income is nearly three times greater than Mexico's. Numbers of people cannot explain overpopulation, either. The United States, with about 310 million people, is quite wealthy. But so is Canada, with only 34 million people. India, with nearly 1.2 billion people, is rather poor, but so are many African countries with small populations.

The key to understanding the idea of overpopulation is culture, or how people live. Do they have a stable democratic government that is responsible to the people and their needs? Do they have a strong free market–based economy? Are people healthy and well educated? If the answer to these questions is "yes," a country is not overpopulated regardless of its population. If the answer is "no," it may suffer overpopulation with even a small number of people. Overpopulated countries are those that have more people than their government, economy, and resources can provide for adequately. This is the problem with Mexico. It has a huge population, living in a small area. It has limited natural resources, little good farmland, a weak economy, and a long history of bad government. All of these factors combine to make Mexico overpopulated.

MEXICAN SETTLEMENT: WHERE PEOPLE LIVE

Population distribution can tell a great deal about a country. When many people live in an area, there is a reason. In some places, plenty of good land and rich soil, enough moisture, and warm temperatures make highly productive farming possible. Large numbers of people are able to feed themselves and their families. In other places, many people cluster around

Many of Mexico's poor live in shacks that border the towns. There are generally no public or social services available to those who inhabit these depressed areas.

rich mineral deposits, large factories, busy seaports, or thriving tourist centers. What such places have in common is that people can find jobs and make a good living.

Population distribution also indicates areas where few people choose to live. In some places, the natural environment may be too poor for farming. In others, there is little industry and there are too few jobs to attract people to the area. Where living is difficult, population is sparse. The natural environment, too, has presented major challenges to settlement. Mexico's landscape has many areas of extremes. Such places are too high or rugged, too wet or dry, too infertile, or in some way too difficult for people to make a good living or to live comfortably. Few people live in such areas. Much of the north and northwest is too dry and too rugged to support large numbers of people. The exception is along the U.S.-Mexico border, where people are drawn by jobs and other opportunities. In the south and southeast, the land is too mountainous and in places too wet to be productive. The Yucatán Peninsula has too meager an environment, with poor soils, little rain much of the year, and no valuable minerals. The area south and east of Mexico's Central Plateau also has too little industry.

The effects of environmental conditions reflect Mexico's population distribution. About 90 percent of the country's people live in a narrow belt that extends from the Pacific Ocean to the Gulf of Mexico and centers on the 20th parallel north latitude and Mexico City. Most large cities are in this belt, including Mexico City (estimated metropolitan area population 24 million), Guadalajara (estimated population 3.5 million), Puebla (estimated population 1.0 million), and Veracruz (estimated population 350,000). Here, soils tend to be fertile and there is ample rainfall for farming. Mining has long been important. Veracruz is Mexico's largest seaport and Mexico City is the social, political, and economic heart of the country. Millions of people can make a living there.

About 77 percent of all Mexicans live in a city. The remaining 23 percent of the country's population is rural, with people living in small farming villages that dot the countryside. These urban/rural figures are almost identical to those of Canada and the United States. The major difference is that Mexico's cities have grown very fast. Mexico City has exploded in population to become one of the world's largest urban centers. Such rapid growth, in a poor country, means that it is not possible to keep pace with the needs for jobs and services. Yet people continue to leave the country and flock to Mexico's cities.

PEOPLE ON THE MOVE

Migration is the movement of people from one place to another. Since the arrival of the Spaniards nearly 500 years ago, Mexico's people have been quite mobile. After the conquest, many native peoples were moved by force. The Catholic Church moved them to villas (small villages) to be able to have better control over the Indians. Huge native populations were moved and forced to work in mines or on farms and ranches, under the encomienda system. Elsewhere, many Indians were forced from their own lands when Spaniards took over the area.

Geographers and other social scientists use the idea of "push-and-pull" factors to help understand migration. When people move, there is a reason they leave. Many things can "push" people into a decision to leave their home. In Mexico, harsh rural living conditions have pushed people from the countryside. There is not enough farmland for the booming population. Most rural people are extremely poor. And in the country and small towns, there is often a lack of important services, such as electricity, clean water, schools, and hospitals.

"Pull" factors help explain where people go and why. Within Mexico, the major pull of the past century has been cities. People believe that cities are exciting and offer an opportunity to better oneself socially and economically. It is easier to live in the city because there are many more services, such as schools, shopping facilities, and medical care. Nearly all of Mexico's cities have grown, and many have exploded in population as people are attracted to them in search of a better life.

During recent decades, several of Mexico's regions have grown because of in-migration (a large-scale influx of people into an area). Many people have moved to the northern desert. Some are drawn by jobs in farming and ranching. But most people move north in search of a different kind of job. Thousands of factories have sprung up during recent decades on the Mexican side of the U.S.–Mexico border. Many people also want to be near the border with a goal of reaching the United States—legally or illegally. Along the Gulf of Mexico, many people have been attracted by jobs in the oil fields.

INTERNATIONAL MIGRATION

A search for better opportunity, particularly economic, is the main reason people move. To outsiders, Mexico has little to offer, and few people choose to migrate there. The country is relatively poor and jobs are scarce. Throughout most of its history, Mexico has been poorly governed. And both corruption and crime have been and continue to be widespread. A small number of Anglo-Americans have retired in Mexico. Others spend a part of the year in the country, usually to enjoy its warmer winter weather. During recent decades, an estimated one million refugees from Central America have crossed the border into Mexico. Many of them are in the country illegally. This has added to Mexico's population and economic burden.

The major migration affecting Mexico's population is to the United States. Mexican workers have been migrating to the United States for 200 years. But today, more are entering the country—legally or illegally—than ever before. In fact, migration from Mexico to the United States is now the greatest flow of migrant workers in the world. It is estimated that as many as 22 million people born in Mexico now live in the United States. With a population of 113 million, this means that about 1 of every 5 native Mexicans now lives in the United States. Many migrants live in the United States legally, and as many as 12 million are undocumented, or are in the country illegally. According to census data, Spanish-speaking people, most of whom are from Mexico, are the largest minority in the United States. In 2010, it was estimated that Hispanics (not all of whom are from Mexico, of course) represent 15.4 percent of the U.S. population, a number that is growing rapidly.

Immigrants climb the border fence between the United States and Mexico and enter the United States illegally to work for low wages, often under harsh conditions.

The boundary between the United States and Mexico is unique. Nowhere else in the world does a wealthy country share such a long and easily penetrated border with a less developed country. Millions of people try to enter the United States illegally each year. Most of them are from Mexico. More than a million of them are caught and returned. Why are they willing to take such a risk?

Undocumented Mexicans are believed to make up more than 5 percent of the U.S. labor force. In some states, the figure is much higher. Some people think that they are taking jobs away from Americans. But others realize that the great majority of jobs held by Mexicans are those that most Americans find undesirable. They are low paying, difficult, and often associated with poor conditions. Why, then, are Mexicans willing to work under these conditions? In the United States, the (2010) legal minimum wage is $7.25 per hour. In Mexico, there is no minimum wage. Jobs are scarce, and many people are willing to work for $7.25 a day, or even less—if they can find work at all.

The average Mexican living in Mexico earns less in one year than many Northern Americans make in one month. If Mexicans can go to the United States and make several thousand dollars, they are able to return home wealthy by Mexican standards. Many Mexicans stay in the United States for only a short period of time. They are called seasonal workers, who return home when they have made what to them is "enough" money.

The flow of workers back and forth between Mexico and the United States has helped both countries. The United States benefits from the many people who are willing to work at hard jobs for low wages. In Mexico, up to 40 percent of working-age people cannot find a permanent, well-paying job. But the 7 to 10 million Mexicans who work in the United States help ease their country's social and economic problems. They boost the Mexican economy by sending millions of American dollars home to help support their families.

WHO ARE THE "MEXICANS"?

Just as there are "many Mexicos," there also are many "Mexicans." The term "Mexican" identifies three general groups of people: Europeans (primarily of Spanish origin), mestizos, and various groups of Amerindians. Many people classify others on the basis of their physical appearance—how they look. Others, including most Mexicans, divide people based on cultural differences, or how they live. Each group has its own way of life. And each sees itself as being different from the others.

Originally, European (Caucasian) and Indian (Mongoloid) were racial terms. A mestizo was someone of mixed European and Indian background, or of mixed race. Most scientists have dropped the idea of race. They realize that human beings are far too mixed to fall into "pure" racial groups. The way people live, after all, is much more important than the way they look.

Today, the terms "European," "mestizo," and "Indian" are often used only to identify cultural, rather than racial, groups. "Mestizo" refers to anyone of Indian background who has accepted Mexico's Hispanic culture (Spanish language, religion, dress, values, and so forth). By changing their way of life, people in Mexico can change their classification. An Indian can become a mestizo simply by accepting the European way of living.

Even though people can move from one level to another, there is a recognized class structure in Mexico. At the top of the social and economic scale are the Europeans, or whites. These people, most of whom trace their ancestry to Spain, number about 10 million (9 percent) of Mexico's population. Throughout most of Mexico's history, they have held the power and most of the wealth. Slightly lower on the socioeconomic scale are the mestizos. Today, about 68 million Mexicans (60 percent) belong to this group. It is often said that mestizos are the "real" Mexicans as seen by Northern Americans. Finally, about 34 million (30 percent) of the population is Native American (Amerindian). Most of these people are poor, living in remote areas and following a very traditional lifestyle. Only about one million of Mexico's people belong to other racial or ethnic groups. There are very small numbers of people who trace their past to Africa, other European countries, or various Asian lands.

As mentioned before, numbers of people alone do not create a condition of overpopulation. The effectiveness of a country's government and economy is of much greater importance in determining how well people live. The next two chapters provide more information about these essential geographic elements.

El Angel de la Independence stands as a monument to Mexico's freedom from Spanish rule in 1821.

6

Political Geography and Government

This chapter discusses the history of Mexico's rocky political geography and the governments that have ruled its people. The view will be broad, with the focus on the important institutions and how they have affected the country's past, molded its present, and will have an impact on its future.

Government and economy are two of the most basic factors that influence the well-being of any country's people. Transportation, communication, education, and health are other important elements of society. Each of these important services, however, depends at least in part on government decisions. And all of them depend on political stability and financial resources that are adequate and dependable.

Mexico has all of the advantages needed to become one of the world's richest and most powerful countries. It has a large, hardworking population, and many of its people are well educated. The country has many natural resources, including a variety of metals and huge petroleum reserves. Mexico is also well on its way to becoming a major industrial power. Of greatest importance, perhaps, it is located next door to the world's largest consumer market, the United States and Canada. Its beautiful and varied natural environment and rich cultural heritage favor Mexico as one of the world's great tourist destinations. To become powerful, however, a country needs many elements to come together. It must have a good government, a strong and cooperative society willing to work for the common good of all, and a healthy economy.

In Mexico, as is true of many countries throughout the world, not everyone shares equally in society's opportunities. Some people are very powerful, while others are powerless. Some people have great wealth, while many live in grinding poverty. These are just two of the problems that Mexico must overcome before it can reach its potential. In this chapter, emphasis focuses on Mexico's government and politics and their roles through time.

MEXICAN INDEPENDENCE

Mexico's past is deeply etched in its present. The country's culture and history help to explain why Mexico has failed to reach its potential. Most of the 300 years of Spanish rule that began when Cortés conquered Tenochtitlán in 1521 were peaceful. But this was also a period of cultural and economic stagnation and decay. The Spanish aristocracy—supported in power by the Spanish military, and the even stronger Roman Catholic Church—strictly controlled society. These two groups held vast power and wealth. They owned much of the productive agricultural land, the mines, and other valuable resources. Most people were powerless and lived in poverty and misery. Slaves did much of the work. Greed, corruption, and illiteracy were widespread. Society was torn apart by suspicion and dislike between groups—European against Indian, various Native American tribal groups against one another, race against race, and rich against poor. Much of Mexico's turbulent history since its independence from Spain can be traced to these roots of conflict.

Mexican independence from Spain was gained with the signing of the Treaty of Córdoba on August 24, 1821. The new country was to be independent from Spain, its religion was to be Roman Catholicism, and its people were to be united, with no division between people on the basis of birth or status.

By 1824, Mexico had a constitution and the country became a republic (a country in which officials are elected by voters). But the Mexican people had almost no experience in governing themselves. Their economy was weak and in decline. For a number of reasons, including the native population's widespread anger against them, most Spaniards had left the country. When they departed, they took much of the country's wealth with them. Their departure also drained Mexico of most of its well-educated, highly trained people. The country fell deeply into debt. There was little money to pay the army, members of which frequently overthrew the government to show their displeasure. For nearly a century, Mexico was in chaos much of the time.

The army, the church, and the wealthy ran the country as they wished. They seldom honored the constitution or other laws. Most Mexicans had no say in how they were ruled. Independence from Spain did not bring democracy. Rather, the earlier harsh and corrupt Spanish colonial rule was simply replaced by the equally bad rule of a handful of wealthy and powerful native-born Mexicans. Governments were so bad and the people were so unhappy that the independent country suffered through 45 different governments during its first 51 years! Most leaders were killed or overthrown from office by the army or by other groups wanting to hold power.

MEXICO'S AREA TAKES SHAPE

During Spanish rule, New Spain (Mexico) reached northward to encompass territory that included nearly a quarter of what is now the United States. Several events caused Mexico to lose this territory during the mid-1800s. Antonio López de Santa Anna was a popular Mexican president. He had defeated a group of Spaniards who, in 1829, were trying to reclaim the country. As a national hero, he was elected president 11 times. But in 1834, Santa Anna declared himself a dictator, took complete control of the government, and threw out the constitution. This caused a violent protest from the people of Texas (which at the time included present-day Texas and parts of New Mexico, Colorado, Kansas, and Wyoming). By 1835, about 7,500 Mexicans lived in Texas, but more than 30,000 people from the United States lived there. Many of the Texans were not Catholic and did not speak Spanish. They resented Mexican control.

On March 2, 1836, Texas declared its independence from Mexico. Within days, Santa Anna led a large army northward into Texas. He attacked rebels who had gathered to defend the Alamo, a mission in San Antonio. The rebels were far outnumbered and were killed during a heroic battle. Texans were outraged. "Remember the Alamo!" became their battle cry. In April, under the leadership of Sam Houston, the Texans took revenge. They attacked the Mexican army at San Jacinto, a site located several miles east of the city that now bears the Texas army leader's name—Houston. This time, Mexican soldiers were no match for the rebels. They fled, and Santa Anna was captured. He was given a choice: death or sign a treaty giving Texas its independence. Given these options, he signed the treaty.

Mexicans were angry over their loss of Texas. And when Texas became a part of the United States in 1845, Mexico and the United States began arguing over the border separating the two countries. By 1846 the disagreement had become heated. U.S. troops moved into a part of Texas that was claimed by

Santa Anna was brought to meet General Sam Houston on April 22, 1836, following Santa Anna's defeat at San Jacinto.

both countries. Historical accounts suggest that Mexican troops opened fire first, giving the United States an excuse to declare war. A bitter war began and raged between the two countries for two years. Mexico was no match for U.S. forces. In 1848 a treaty was signed placing the boundary between Texas (by that time, part of the United States) and Mexico at the Rio Grande. The United States also gained California, Nevada, Utah, and parts of present-day Arizona, Wyoming, Colorado, and New Mexico. The United States paid Mexico $15 million for the land that it gained. It was a tremendous bargain. Today, the states occupying territory gained from Mexico produce several hundred times the area's original purchase price—*each day*—in agricultural and manufactured goods, natural resources, and services.

In 1853, Mexico lost the final piece of land that became part of the United States. The United States bought a thin sliver of territory that is now part of southern Arizona and New

Mexico. This $10 million deal is known in the United States as the Gadsden Purchase. By 1853 the map of present-day Mexico had taken shape. But the once huge country had lost more than three-quarters of its formerly held territory.

REVOLUTION AND REFORM

By the dawn of the 1900s, Mexico was ripe for revolution. The country had been ruled for a quarter century by a ruthless dictator. Much of Mexico's wealth—including its natural resources, agriculture, and trade—was controlled by foreigners. In Mexico, people who owned large parcels of land had grown even more powerful. Fewer than 1,000 families owned nearly half of the country's best land. Some rich landowners owned more than 2 million acres (809,400 hectares). One of them, Luis Terrazas, became one of the world's largest individual landowners. His ranch, located in the northern state of Chihuahua, covered 7 million acres, or 2.83 million hectares (an area about the size of Massachusetts). On the huge ranch, he grazed some 500,000 cattle and 250,000 sheep. Two-thousand vaqueros (cowboys) watched over the herds using the ranch's 25,000 horses and 5,000 mules. At the opposite extreme, more than 3 million rural families (96 percent of the rural farm population) did not even own the land on which they lived and worked.

Revolution finally erupted in 1910. At its heart was the need for redistribution of land and opportunity. Yet another dictator, Porfirio Díaz, was overthrown, resulting in seven years of political chaos. During this period, no strong central government was in control. Personal armies of regional leaders fought one another in a destructive struggle that nearly tore the country apart. Two leaders of the revolution were Emiliano Zapata and Pancho Villa. Zapata was joined by many farmers, to whom he said, "It is better to die on your feet than to live on your knees." Pancho Villa became known as the "Robin Hood of Mexico." He took from the rich and

Francisco "Pancho" Villa led rebels in the Revolution of 1910 against the government and wealthy landowners.

gave to the poor. In 1917 these men and other leaders gained support for a new constitution.

The new constitution included many reforms. It also brought political stability to the country that has continued to the present day. Under the new constitution, a president could serve only one six-year term, with no possibility of reelection. Limits were placed on the ownership of property by both the Roman Catholic Church and foreigners. Everyone was to have access to free schools. Workers were to receive fair wages, and they were allowed to form labor unions. Of all the changes, perhaps none was more important than land reform.

GROWING NATIONAL UNITY

Even with its new constitution and government, Mexico still faced many serious problems. It had to find ways to give its poor people more opportunity and freedom. And it had to draw people of different races and cultures together. People had to begin thinking of themselves as being Mexicans, rather than holding ties to individual regions, leaders, or tribes. This was largely accomplished through four approaches.

The first approach was land division. Some way had to be found to give people who worked small plots of land control over the land they farmed. This was done through a massive land redistribution program. Beginning in 1917, about half of Mexico's farmland was redistributed. The land was taken from owners of the huge haciendas (estates) and legally transferred to small farming communities, called *ejidos*. Today, each of Mexico's more than 28,000 ejidos is a farming village of 20 or more families. The government owns the land, but each village and each farmer can use the land as if it was their own. The program has been successful.

The second approach was to make public education available to everyone. Today, education is free and students are required to attend school through nine grades. Fifty years ago, only about half of Mexico's people could read and write. Today, the number has risen to more than 95 percent. Mexico also has many fine universities and trade schools. The National Autonomous University in Mexico City has almost 300,000 students. It is the largest university in the Western Hemisphere and one of the largest in the world.

The third approach was to glorify Mexico's Indian heritage. Throughout the country, many museums, monuments, and murals emphasize the importance of Mexico's rich American Indian culture and history. Today, regardless of their race or culture, most Mexicans take great pride in their country's native heritage.

The final approach to drawing Mexico together was to create a single political party. In 1917 the Institutional Revolutionary Party, better known by the Spanish acronym PRI (Partido Revolucionario Institucional), was formed. In 1929 the party was chosen to lead the country. Under the PRI, Mexico became a one-party democracy. People could vote for their leaders, but there was only one major party from which they could choose. For nearly 70 years, most people were happy. The PRI claimed to be the party of the poor. It also favored labor, farmers, and business. By 2000 the PRI had been in power for seven decades. No other political party in the world had held on to power for as long a time.

Each of these four strategies helped Mexico become more unified. Today the country's people think of themselves as being "Mexicans" and take pride in their nation. By giving all of its people greater opportunity, by taking pride in its past, and by developing and maintaining a democratic government, Mexico has become a unified nation.

TRUE DEMOCRACY COMES TO MEXICO

Even though one political party, the PRI, had ruled Mexico since 1929, in an election held in July 2000, the "unthinkable" happened. For the first time in the country's history, Mexico peacefully changed political parties in a democratic way. The new president, Vicente Fox, was the National Action Party (PAN) candidate.

For years, the PRI had been accused of many kinds of corruption. People became tired of the ruling party's favoritism, bribery, and many other dishonest practices. They wanted change. But many people worried what might happen if the PRI was voted out of power. They thought that many of the gains made under the party's control would be lost. The election of 2000 went smoothly. So did the transition of governments. Mexico entered the twenty-first century as a mature democracy with a seemingly bright political future. For the first time in memory, voters can select candidates from more than a single political party.

A ROCKY POLITICAL ROAD AHEAD?

Governing Mexico has never been easy, and many people believe that the country faces a rocky political road ahead. During the latter part of the first decade of the twenty-first century, the country's economy entered a huge slump. Oil production, the source of about 40 percent of Mexico's revenue, dropped sharply as deposits began to run dry. Toward the end of the decade, the price of oil also plunged from its earlier high. Crime, much of which is drug-related, is rampant. The country has one of the world's highest rates of murder and kidnapping. Between 2006 and the end of 2010, more than 30,000 people are believed to have been killed in drug-related violence. At least seven major drug cartels operate in Mexico today. According to some estimates, more than half of Mexico's 31 states have fallen under their control. When this happens, they infiltrate and control the police, judicial system, and increasingly, the government itself. Once a government is corrupted, it is very difficult to "clean up" and restore honesty and integrity.

Many Mexicans are unhappy with the way their country is headed. Of course, they blame their political leaders. In the 2009 midterm election, the PRI—the party that governed

Mexico for seven decades—did extremely well. It doubled its seats in the lower house of Congress, its candidates won five of six contested state governorships, and many PRI candidates won elections for mayorships. All things considered, it appears that Mexico still has a long way to go before democracy flourishes and stability is established.

Mexico faces many problems as the country attempts to move from a traditional rural society to a modern industrial nation. Rugged terrain, poor transportation facilities, and isolation are among the problems that somehow must be overcome before these communities can be drawn into the modern world. Here, Mexican laborers work in a cross-border *maquiladora* plant.

CHAPTER

7

An Awakening Economic Giant

A country's economy is measured by all the resources it has and uses, the goods its people produce, and all of the services that its people provide. Also important are the ways by which goods and services are distributed to the people. Mexico has a wealth of natural and human resources. Some people believe that it should be one of the most wealthy and powerful countries in the world. Yet Mexico's full economic potential has never been reached. The country remains a sleeping economic giant. Both Mexico and an alarming number of its people remain quite poor. But there are many signs that it is awakening. This chapter reviews the problems that have limited Mexico's economic growth and highlights the vast potentials that this land and its people possess.

PROBLEMS OF DEVELOPMENT

There are many reasons Mexico's economy has been slow to develop. The following list spotlights problems the country must overcome in order to grow economically. It will be helpful to compare conditions in the United States with those in Mexico. This will explain why it is so difficult for a country to develop economically.

Mexico had a wealth of natural resources on which its early economy could have been built, particularly its rich supply of silver and gold. But these precious metals were controlled by Spain, and it was that country that benefited from them. Until recently, most Mexicans depended on farming, rather than manufacturing, for their living. Building a modern industrial economy that involves a balance of manufacturing, commerce, and services takes a long time and a tremendous amount of capital. Mexico is beginning to develop, but it still has a long way to go.

In some ways, one of Mexico's greatest problems is the sixteenth-century Mediterranean "baggage" that it inherited from Spain. With the Spanish conquest, New Spain (Mexico) took on many of Spain's social and cultural traditions. Some of these traditions have been difficult to break. One is the belief that hard physical labor is to be avoided by "gentlemen." Another problem is a class system in which a small number of people hold nearly all of the wealth and power. Most economically developed countries have a large middle class, with smaller numbers of wealthy and poor. In Mexico, the middle class is very small. Additionally, a long tradition of corruption, also a Mediterranean trait, has slowed economic development.

If a country's economy is to grow, people must be willing to invest their money in its development. Mexico's many political, social, and economic problems have discouraged investment. Few people—whether from Mexico or other countries—are willing to invest their money in a country that is not stable.

Without such investment, there simply is not enough money to build such essential things as factories, businesses, tourist facilities, and transportation linkages.

Government plays an important role in economic development. It can either help or severely hinder a country's chances to grow economically. Mexico has a mixed record. At times, the government has encouraged development. During the late 1800s, for example, the country experienced huge economic growth thanks to government efforts. But foreigners controlled much of the growth and held much of the wealth. During much of the 1900s, government ownership and control of many businesses hurt the economy. So did trade barriers that imposed huge taxes on imported items. One of the worst problems is "red tape." It takes three to four times as many steps to do business in Mexico as it does in the United States. Many companies simply become discouraged and go elsewhere.

During much of its history, Mexico's population growth has outstripped its economic development. Its people therefore became poorer each year. Today, nearly one million people enter the country's workforce annually. This means that one million new jobs must be created each year just to stay even. During recent years, population growth has slowed. This will help put Mexico in a better position to experience future economic growth and development.

If people do not have money, they cannot buy things and the economy suffers. Mexico must improve the distribution of and access to money. The richest 10 percent of all Mexicans control nearly 40 percent of the country's wealth. The poorest 10 percent control only 1.7 percent of the wealth. Nearly half of Mexico's population is too poor to buy many of the things they need. The country also must improve its access to money. Wages are very low. Many Mexicans must work a full day or longer to earn what a person in Canada or the United States makes in one hour. Finally, high interest rates make it very costly to borrow money.

One of the most important geographic features of any country is its transportation network—the means and routes by which people, materials, and goods are transported from place to place. Because of Mexico's rugged terrain, building highways and railroads is very costly. Many areas even today do not have adequate transportation linkages. Even where they exist, railroads are inefficient and many highways are in poor condition. Modern toll roads built in more populated areas are too expensive for many Mexicans to use.

As Mexico begins to develop its manufacturing and other kinds of business, it faces heavy competition. Particularly in Asia, home to more than half of the world's people, many countries have become heavily industrialized. Their people, like those of Mexico, are willing to work for relatively low wages. Think of the products—clothing, electronics and appliances, vehicles, and many others—that Northern American families own. How many of them are from Asian countries? How many are from Mexico?

A former Mexican president said, "[The drug trade] has become the most serious threat to our national security, our society's health, and civic peace." There is a great fear in Mexico that the drug trade will grow to control both the country's government and its economy. In some areas of the country and sections of the economy, conditions suggest that this has already happened.

"So far from God," a popular Mexican saying goes, "[and] so close to the United States." The country's location is, indeed, a mixed blessing. On the positive side, there are at least three advantages. First, the United States and Canada are Mexico's major trading partners. This makes trade easier and less expensive. Second, because the United States and Mexico are neighbors, Northern Americans find it easier to understand and work with Mexicans than might be the case with people from a more distant land and culture. Third, many Mexicans (both legal and undocumented) find work in the United States. In fact, remittances (money sent by Mexicans living in the United States, Canada, or elsewhere to relatives in Mexico) make up the country's third-greatest source of legal income. It is topped only by oil and tourism.

The major downside to Mexico's location has to do with the way the country is judged in comparison to its larger, more powerful neighbor. The U.S. economy is the world's largest. No matter how much Mexico's economy develops, it will rank poorly in comparison to that of the United States. A comparison with other Latin American countries is much more meaningful. Recently, the Mexican economy surpassed that of Brazil on a per capita basis, thereby overtaking Latin America's leading economic powerhouse in that important category.

PROSPECTS FOR GROWTH

Mexico appears to be on the brink of potentially explosive economic growth. There are signs that many of the problems listed above are being overcome. A number of key industries are growing, thereby creating more and better jobs and greater opportunities in sales and services as well. The country's middle class is growing. Recent elections proved that democracy can work in Mexico. If this continues, the country should experience stability that will encourage investment. Since 2006, the government has taken steps to fight corruption in all forms, including the huge illegal drug trade.

Transportation is improving. And Mexico's rate of population growth is slowing. Of greatest importance, perhaps, are two recent programs that have more closely linked Mexico's economy to that of its Northern American neighbors, the United States and Canada.

THE NORTH AMERICAN FREE TRADE AGREEMENT (NAFTA)

Mexico's economy—including about 85 percent of its exports and 50 percent of its imports—is very closely tied to those of its giant northern neighbors, the United States and Canada. The North American Free Trade Agreement, or NAFTA, opens the door to freer trade between Mexico and Northern America. It is supposed to cut restrictions and remove tariffs (taxes). The program began in January 1994 and was scheduled to lead to completely free trade between the three countries by 2009.

Some people see NAFTA as a form of economic salvation. Others see it as a threat. Even the countries involved often see the good and bad sides of NAFTA differently. Mexico, for example, gained many more jobs. But in Canada and the United States, some people complain that their jobs have been lost to Mexico because people there are willing to work for lower wages. Mexicans see the thousands of new factories and millions of new jobs as good. But some people worry about the environmental pollution caused by the factories. In Mexico, shoppers find many more goods in their stores. In the United States, there is hope that NAFTA-created jobs in Mexico will slow the flood of illegal migrants.

It is still too early to judge fully the success of NAFTA. Some interests in each of the countries involved no doubt will be hurt by free trade. But many others will benefit. It seems safe to say that overall, NAFTA has done much more good than harm. Certainly it has increased the importance of Mexico's location next to its rich Northern American neighbors.

MAQUILADORAS

A second program has brought more than 3,000 manufacturing industries and some 1.3 million workers to Mexico's border with the United States. Americans or Canadians own many of these factories, called *maquiladoras* (assembly plants). They operate in Mexico using foreign (primarily Northern American) parts, capital (money and equipment), technology, and often management. Mexicans provide the land and labor. Most parts are manufactured in the United States or elsewhere and shipped to factories on the Mexican side of the U.S.–Mexico border, where they are assembled. Foreign firms benefit from low labor costs and (under the rules established by NAFTA) no import tariffs for goods crossing the U.S., Canadian, and Mexican borders. Mexico benefits from the many jobs created by the maquiladoras. Although workers earn wages about one-sixth those of comparable laborers in the United States, for Mexicans they are relatively high.

NAFTA and the maquiladoras are just two of the many developments that have helped Mexico's economy grow during recent decades. The country has a broadly developed base of primary and secondary industries and a rapidly expanding tertiary (service) industry upon which further development can be built.

MEXICO'S ECONOMIC BASE

Economic activity can be divided into several basic types that include primary, secondary, and tertiary industries. The following brief survey of Mexico's economic development follows this framework.

Primary Industries

A primary industry is one that is closely tied to the earth and its land, water, mineral, plant, and animal resources. For centuries, nearly all of Mexico's economic activity depended upon extraction of its natural resources, particularly precious metals. Today, mining, agriculture, fishing, and the lumber industry are still important. But with the exception of the oil industry, their contribution to the country's gross domestic product (GDP) is less than 5 percent.

Of the various primary industries, mining and oil are the most important. In fact, Mexico ranks as one of the world's leading countries in the production of minerals. It has rich deposits of copper, lead, zinc, and iron and continues to rank first in the production of silver.

Some 3,000 maquiladoras—factories on the Mexican side of the border—provide jobs for more than one million Mexican laborers. These plants use Anglo-American parts and employ Mexican labor at low wages to finish manufactured goods that are returned to the United States and Canada.

Mexico also has extensive petroleum deposits and ranks seventh among the world's producers, with an estimated 4 to 5 percent of proven world reserves and a comparable level of production. Nearly all oil comes from fields discovered in 1976 that border on the Gulf of Mexico or from offshore wells located within the gulf. The United States buys most of the petroleum that Mexico itself does not use. During recent years, Pemex, the state-owned oil company, has contributed nearly 40 percent of Mexico's federal revenues. The company is also the country's single largest employer, with nearly 139,000 workers.

Agriculture, as it has been for centuries, continues to be an important economic activity. Approximately 14 percent of the country's population is engaged in farming or ranching, and agriculture accounts for about 4 percent of the country's wealth. The reason for the 10-point span between population and wealth can easily be explained. Some 14 million Mexicans are subsistence farmers. That is, they grow only enough for their own family and perhaps a few items for sale in a local market. Ranching, introduced by the early Spaniards, continues to be important throughout much of the country. Sugarcane is an important cash crop along the coast of the Gulf of Mexico. In the northern desert, cotton is grown on huge irrigated farms. Because of the warmer climate, many irrigated farms in northern Mexico also grow fruit and vegetables for U.S. winter markets.

Fishing and logging are locally important in a number of areas. The waters of the Pacific teem with marine life, including many valuable species of fish and shellfish. Commercial fishing centers dot the coast, and many communities, particularly on the Baja Peninsula and the mainland coast of the Gulf of California, have developed as tourist centers supported by a lively sport fishing industry. Fishing is also important in the Gulf of Mexico, which is particularly well known for its shrimp, clams, oysters, and crabs. As for the logging industry, extensive deforestation has occurred throughout much of Mexico. Today, commercial lumbering is limited to more remote, often mountainous, areas.

Secondary Industries

Nearly 25 percent of the Mexican labor force is engaged in secondary industries. These are activities that process, change, or manufacture raw materials produced by primary industries. Thousands of manufacturing plants are located in and around Mexico City, the country's economic hub. Along the coast of the Gulf of Mexico, refineries in Villahermosa and elsewhere produce gasoline from crude oil. Monterrey, in northeastern Mexico, is home to the country's largest steel mill.

The largest and most productive industrial region, however, is that formed by the band of maquiladoras that stretch from coast to coast along the U.S.–Mexico border. From Tijuana, on the Pacific Ocean south of San Diego, California, to Matamoros, near the mouth of the Rio Grande south of Brownsville, Texas, these factories have boosted the region's economy. These "border towns" and others like them—Mexicali, Nogales, Ciudad Juarez, and Nuevo Laredo, to name but a few—have shown explosive growth during the recent decades. People have flocked to the border from throughout Mexico to find jobs in these plants.

Tertiary Industries

Nearly two-thirds of Mexico's workforce is engaged in tertiary, or service-related, industries. These include sales, tourist-related activities, teaching, the health services, communications and transportation, and entertainment industries. Since people engaged in these activities serve other people, such industries are concentrated in population centers. Mexico City, for example, is home to perhaps half of all service-related jobs.

Tourism is a major contributor to Mexico's economy, accounting for about 13 percent of the country's GDP. In fact, Mexico ranks as the number one tourist destination in all of Latin America. Millions of people from all over the world flock to Mexico's fascinating cities, quaint villages, splendid archaeological sites, and world-class coastal resorts. Cancún, on the eastern coast of the Yucatán Peninsula, has become one of the most popular coastal tourist destinations in the world. Its sandy beaches, the warm and sparkling clear waters of the Caribbean, and dozens of hotels and other tourist facilities make it an ideal year-round playground. Acapulco and Puerto Vallarta are popular tourist destinations on the mountainous Pacific coast. During recent decades, the government has encouraged the development of other tourist destinations, ensuring that this important contributor to the nation's economy will continue to grow.

Inland cities also attract tourists. Mexico City—with its many archaeological, cultural, economic, and historical benefits, plus an international airport, excellent shopping, countless hotels, and other tourist amenities—welcomes more visitors than any other location in the country. But dozens of other cities—from the U.S.–Mexican border towns that attract tourists with low prices, to the Yucatán Peninsula with its many Mayan sites—also offer excitement and fun for the tourist.

Although recent years have been quite difficult in terms of Mexico's economy, there are major signs of improvement. The long-slumbering economic giant is beginning to stir.

Pilgrims carry the image of the Virgin of Guadalupe at the Basilica of Guadalupe in Mexico City. Thousands of people from all over the country converge on the basilica, bringing images to be blessed on the Day of the Virgin of Guadalupe.

CHAPTER

8

Living in Mexico Today

S ome Mexicans continue to live in very traditional ways, as did their Indian ancestors centuries ago. Many Mexicans, however, enjoy a completely modern lifestyle. Nearly everyone in Mexico shares ways of living that link their culture's present to the past. Native cultures cling to many of their traditional ways of living. For example, social interactions, the houses in which they live, the languages they speak, and the foods they eat may be little changed from those of their distant ancestors. People of Spanish heritage live much like their distant ancestors in Spain. Mestizo people live in the world of both native and Spanish cultures. For most Mexicans, however, daily life is a blend of both Spanish European and Native American Indian ways of living. Language, religion, and customs, for example, show strong links to the Spanish past. But many words, crops, foods, and customs are drawn from the country's proud native heritage.

CHANGING WAYS OF LIVING

There is little truth to the image of Mexico as a sleepy, backward nation of rural farmers struggling to survive. Today, three of every four Mexicans live in a town or city. For most Mexicans, the siesta (afternoon nap) is but a pleasant memory of an earlier and more relaxed lifestyle. Nine of every ten residents can read and write. The standard of living for most people has improved greatly during recent decades. In many ways, Mexican culture and society are undergoing huge changes—from a folk (traditional) culture to a popular (modern, urban, educated) culture. For most Mexicans, the lifestyle in modern Mexico is much more like that of many developed countries than it is of the world's poorer nations.

The Human Development Index (HDI) is a United Nations measure of human well-being. It takes into consideration many factors, including life expectancy, education and literacy, and other indices of a country's standard of living. Mexico ranks fifty-sixth among the world's countries, but among mainland Latin American countries, only Chile, Argentina, Uruguay, and Panama rank higher. (The 2010 HDI ranked the United States fourth and Canada eighth.)

During the past 50 years, Mexico has experienced a cultural revolution. Much of its Indian and mestizo population has made the change from traditional folk culture to modern popular culture in just one or two generations. Such change is often difficult. Imagine what life was like for people in previous generations in remote villages. They did not read or write. Everything they used they made themselves—houses, clothing, and tools. They grew all of their own food. Their villages had no electricity, sewage system, or water piped to homes. There was no television or radio. They knew little of the world beyond. Their lives were influenced by many superstitions. When they were ill, they used various folk remedies—clay, roots, herbs, and other "cures."

Today, many Mexican people live in huge modern cities. They attend school and enjoy reading and writing. Everything that they use and eat is purchased. They cannot imagine living without television, a radio, a CD player, and a computer. A plane can carry them across the country or whisk them across either of its bordering oceans to Europe or Asia in less than a day. Even if they have not traveled far, they are aware of countless other places, people, and conditions. Science, rather than superstition, provides them with many answers. Doctors are available to prescribe the most modern medicines. Think about some of the problems that might be experienced for families that make this cultural "leap" in one or two generations.

CULTURAL TIES

Language, religion, and a number of attitudes and customs can help tie a culture together. In studying Mexican culture, it is important to remember that at the time of conquest, and for more than a thousand years before, Mexico was home to some of the most developed cultures on Earth. Much of this rich native way of life and the landscapes that it created were destroyed by the Spanish conquerors. Spanish-introduced ways of living dominate much of today's Mexican culture. But many native practices continue to be important. Mexican Spanish has been strongly influenced by Amerindian languages. Much of Mexico's food, dress, architecture, arts, and folkways also show a strong Indian imprint. This blend of Spanish and Native Amerindian culture has given modern Mexico a culture unlike any other in the world.

LANGUAGE

Spanish is Mexico's official language and is spoken by 93 percent of the population. About 6 percent of the population speaks one or more of nearly 100 Amerindian languages, including Mayan and Nahuatl (Aztec). Nearly all people who speak an Indian tongue also speak some Spanish. Many Mexicans also speak English, which has become an important second language for those engaged in international business and travel, or who are involved in science or modern technology. Many young people are eager to learn English. It is becoming the international language of the media—music, television, movies, books, magazines, and the Internet.

Language shows movement, the flow of words from one culture to another. Mexican Spanish, for example, has adopted many words from English. In Mexico City, it would not be at all strange to hear someone ordering a *hamburgeresa,* taking a "coffee break," or answering a question with "Okay!"

Hundreds of Spanish words, many from Mexico, have entered the English language. For example, *sierra* (mountain range), *mesa* (table), and *arroyo* (small, dry gully) are used to identify landform features. Mexican words for food include *tacos, tamales, enchiladas, chili,* and *salsa.* Northern Americans may have seen a *rodeo,* a spirited *palomino mustang* bucking, or perhaps a *bronco* confined in a *corral.* Still other words refer to entertainment, such as a *fiesta* in a *plaza, guitar* music, and *mariachi* singers. Each of these words is a reminder of the importance of the cultural exchange of terms.

Spanish words play another important role in the geography of the United States. Hundreds of places and features have Spanish names. El Paso (the pass), Las Vegas (the meadows), San Diego and San Francisco (named for saints), and Los Angeles (the angels) are just some such cities.

RELIGION

The religious conquest of Mexico began in 1523. Just two years after the Aztec capital of Tenochtitlán fell to Cortés, the first Roman Catholic missionaries arrived. They immediately began to learn the Amerindian languages. And they studied the history, customs, and religious practices of Mexico's native peoples. Soon, they were able to begin teaching Christianity. So successful were the missionaries that today more than three of every four Mexicans is Roman Catholic.

The church has played an important role in Mexico's history. Early missionaries settled many Mexican towns and cities as villas. In these communities, Indians were taught Christianity, but they learned many other things as well. Many new crops, including wheat, were introduced. The priests introduced cattle and horses to the Indians and also introduced many new farming techniques.

Over the centuries, the church became very powerful. It owned much of the best land. It also had a very strong influence on Mexico's culture, economy, and government. Many people were unhappy with the church's control. When Mexico's constitution was written, power was shifted from the Catholic Church to the government and people. The constitution guaranteed freedom of worship. But it did not allow the church to own property or be directly involved in government affairs. It also banned church schools. Even though outlawed, in a country where the government was too poor to have enough schools for its people, the church continued to play an important role in education.

Today, the Catholic Church is no longer as strong as it once was. Few people attend church services. Throughout Mexico, however, earlier church influence on culture, history, and beliefs is apparent even today. Churches dominate the landscape of many communities; cemeteries occupy vast areas of space; and many Catholic holidays continue to be widely celebrated.

The Virgin of Guadalupe is Mexico's patron saint. On a cold December morning in 1531, Juan Diego was walking to church to attend Mass. Suddenly, as legend goes, he was blinded by light and heard the sound of strange music. Before him appeared a dark-skinned woman. Calling Juan "my son," she said that she was the Virgin Mary, mother of Christ. According to the legend, she made several appearances before him. Many

Catholics doubted Juan Diego's story. But the Virgin, according to legend, appeared once again. She told Juan Diego to pick roses that he would find growing on a cold, dry, rocky hillside. He gathered the beautiful blossoms in his cloak and took them to the bishop. When he opened the cloak to show the roses, a perfect image of the dark-skinned Virgin Mary appeared.

Juan Diego's cloak, showing what has come to be known as the *Virgen de Guadalupe*, has been preserved. Nearly five centuries later, the image remains clearly imprinted. Each year, on December 12, millions of Mexicans gather for prayers, parades, and fireworks to honor the Virgin of Guadalupe, Mexico's patron saint and national symbol.

HOMES

It is not possible to describe a "typical" Mexican home. Each Amerindian group created its own unique type of buildings. Local materials—wood, clay, or stone—were (and often still are) used in ways that are deeply set in the traditions of each culture. Native houses may appear to be "primitive," but often they are better designed for their environment than are modern homes.

Differences in folk housing (houses built by traditional rural folk) contribute greatly to the regional character of rural Mexico. Because each culture creates its own unique housing landscape, geographers and others often use buildings to identify the regional distribution of folk cultures. Modern houses, whether in the city or the country, also show great differences. Today, income and owner preference, rather than traditional culture, are the major factors determining the kind of house in which one lives.

Many of Mexico's larger cities are surrounded by barrios (slum settlements). Here, people live in extreme poverty. Their homes are crude shacks, often nothing more than cardboard crates thrown together. Few of the houses have running water or electricity. Dirt streets turn to mud after rains. Homes of the

Mexico is a country steeped in history and presenting many contrasts. In Mexico City, the cultural evolution is reflected in ancient Aztec ruins, a centuries-old colonial-era church, and modern apartment buildings.

wealthy often are found within the inner city. This pattern is opposite that of most U.S. cities, where the inner city is often home to the poor, and the wealthy live on the outer edges of the city or in suburbs. Many homes are heavily protected. High surrounding walls may be topped with sharp, jagged pieces of broken glass or razor-sharp barbed wire. Windows may be covered with iron bars to give further protection. Another difference is that in Mexico, the poor tend to live on higher slopes, whereas in Northern America the wealthy tend to occupy higher elevations that offer sweeping views.

FOOD

As is true of nearly everything else in Mexico, food is marked by great variety. Each culture and each region has its own unique diet. The "Mexican" food with which most Americans are familiar is based on the diet of native cultures and the rural poor, particularly from Mexico's northern states. Therefore, it is not the traditional food of people who frequently eat in restaurants. Only in the United States (and more recently in Canada and a few other countries) has Mexico's traditional rural diet become commercially popular. The "Mexican-American," or "Tex-Mex," food served in Anglo-American restaurants would hardly be recognized in Mexico. Many different ingredients have been added and new foods have been created.

Mexico's history and cultures are tasted in its food. The country's diet is mainly a blend of Indian and Spanish traditions. But it was also influenced by French, African, Caribbean, and more recently, Northern American crops and cooking. The blending has resulted in one of the world's most distinctive, most complex, and most delicious cuisines.

Before the conquest, most Amerindians had a diet based on maize, beans, squash, and hot peppers. These foods were usually eaten combined with spices, vegetables, and meat or seafood. Tortillas—flat, round, cakes made from corn flour—were eaten at every meal. From region to region, many other foods were important. The native diet included peanuts, avocados, and tomatoes. Vanilla, chocolate, and honey were used to make drinks and to add flavor to some dishes.

With the arrival of the Spaniards, many more foods became available. The Europeans brought wheat, and many natives began to develop a preference for tortillas made from wheat flour. Spaniards preferred white bread. They also brought rice, which became very popular, particularly in the warm, humid, coastal lowlands. Onions, garlic, and many different Old World vegetables were also introduced. Each of these crops is widely used in Mexican cooking today. The Spaniards also brought citrus trees—orange, lemon, lime, and grapefruit—to Mexico. Grapes were introduced and used to make wine for Roman Catholic religious services. Beef, pork, lamb, and chicken were added to the diet, as were milk and cheese. Many newly introduced spices also added zest to the region's cooking.

Mole poblano, Mexico's most honored recipe, is typical of the country's fancy dishes. It blends Amerindian and Spanish ingredients, it takes hours to make, and it will not be found in any but the best Anglo-American "Mexican" restaurants. Mole poblano is a rich, thick sauce that is usually used with turkey, chicken, or pork. It includes several kinds of peppers (each of which has a different flavor and level of hotness) and can have several dozen ingredients. The actual ingredients used vary regionally and, of course, most cooks have their own secret recipe. One popular recipe calls for five kinds of peppers, garlic, onions, tomatoes, almonds, peanuts, cloves, peppercorns, cinnamon, aniseed, raisins, salt, sugar, sesame seeds, and unsweetened (cooking) chocolate. The key ingredient that makes mole poblano different from other Mexican sauces is the dominant taste of its bitter chocolate.

Today, food preferences of Mexico's middle and upper classes are changing. White bread is replacing corn and wheat tortillas. Soft drinks are replacing traditional fruit juices. Throughout Mexico, norteamericano fast-food restaurants have introduced hamburgers, fried chicken, pizza, and—yes— even Tex-Mex Mexican fast food, all of which have become very popular. Many modern-day Mexicans do not even like the burning taste of hot sauce.

ATTITUDES AND CUSTOMS

Each culture has its own values and ways of believing and behaving. Mexicans, like many other cultures, place a very high value on family, honesty, personal honor, friendship, and humor. In business, a person's word or handshake can seal a deal. To go back on one's word would blemish the family name and reputation and bring dishonor to the individual.

Tastes in food have changed and new ingredients have been introduced over the years, but tortillas made of corn flour are still kneaded and baked over fire in villages throughout the country.

Most Mexicans are patriotic and proud of their country. They also possess a powerful self-image. Machismo is an attitude and behavior held by many Mexican men. It is the idea of a man being strong, forceful, and attractive to women.

In years past, most Mexicans enjoyed a rather slow pace of life. The custom of taking a siesta, an after-lunch nap, was widely practiced throughout the country. Many clock-watching Northern Americans are critical of the Mexicans' attitude toward time. They become impatient with Mexicans who have a *"mañana"* (tomorrow) attitude toward getting things done. And they are critical when Mexicans are late for appointments. Many of these traditional Mexican attitudes and customs are changing as the country's population becomes more urbanized. For a people who, over a span of centuries, lived by sunrise, the solar zenith (peak in the sky during daily passage), and sundown, punctuality measured by hours, minutes, and seconds is of little importance.

Attitudes and customs of other cultures often seem strange to outsiders. And, unfortunately, people are often critical of behavior they do not understand. It is important, therefore, to look closely at another culture to better understand why things are done a certain way. Nearly always, when practices are viewed this way, things that once seemed "strange" begin to make perfect sense. Through knowledge comes understanding, and with understanding comes acceptance. Perhaps this is the single most important reason for studying geography.

Several Mexican attitudes and customs may appear to be strange to most readers: trusting others on their word, machismo, the slow pace of life, taking an afternoon siesta, and the lack of attention to time. If one understands Mexican culture, however, they won't seem so strange. For example, there is a code of trust in Mexico, and it is not unusual for a deal to be sealed with a handshake instead of lawyers and contracts.

Machismo is a behavior found among men throughout much of Mediterranean Europe. Rather than bragging, as it may appear to outsiders, it is an expression of self-confidence. Those cultures believe that to be successful, a man must believe in himself.

A slow pace of life is something common to nearly all traditional cultures. City living, competition, and jobs, on the other hand, call for schedules and a frantic pace. Most people, given the opportunity, would like to slow down and enjoy life more fully.

Finally, the siesta is often pointed to as "proof" of Mexicans' laziness. Yet nothing could be farther from the truth. In traditional Mexico, because of the heat, the workday often begins very early. It is not at all uncommon for men to be in their fields and women working in their home by 4:00 or 5:00 A.M. In the cities, many shops stay open late. For rural people, the noon meal is usually the largest of the day (a practice that is much healthier than eating the largest meal in the evening).

After having worked for many hours and eating a large meal, taking a nap makes perfectly good sense. Also, the early to mid-afternoon "siesta time" is the hottest part of the day, and most of Mexico is in a tropical or subtropical climate. By mid-afternoon, people return to the fields or shops and, well rested, often work well into the evening. The evening meal may not be served until 8:00 P.M. or later. Explaining regional customs and attitudes makes those traits seem much less strange.

SPORTS

The most popular sport in Mexico is *fútbol* (soccer). Whether played in the huge Mexico City stadium before a crowd of 100,000 people or on the dirt streets of a small mountain village, everyone in the country seems to love playing or watching fútbol. Bullfighting is also popular. Many people criticize this activity because of its cruelty to the animals. But it is the country's second most popular sport, and some of Mexico's greatest heroes have been famous *toreadors* (bullfighters). Baseball, basketball, wrestling, and boxing are also popular. Mexico City hosted the Summer Olympic Games in 1968, and in 1986 the country hosted the soccer World Cup competition.

HOLIDAYS

Mexico has many national and religious holidays. Most of them are celebrated much as are holidays in Northern America. Some of the holidays draw families and friends together. On religious holidays, the church or other religious shrines or practices serve as the focus of attention and activity. Still other holidays observe the country's heritage and draw people together for public celebration. New Year's Day, Easter, and Christmas are all celebrated as they are in the United States. Other important holidays include Constitution Day (February 5); the birthday of Benito Juarez, first Indian to govern Mexico (March 21); Cinco de Mayo, celebrating Mexico's victory over France in 1867 (May 5); Independence Day (September 16); Columbus Day (October 12); Revolution Day, recognizing the Mexican

Revolution of 1910 (November 20); and Day of the Virgin of Guadalupe (December 12).

THE FAMILY

The family is the basic unit of Mexican society. Family members may have more than one name; take for example a name like Juan Carlos Espinosa Garcia. In this example, Espinosa comes from the father's family name and Garcia from that of the mother. The first "last" name is used on most occasions, the second being used only for formal or legal identification. Polite greetings identify an individual as *Señor* (Mr.), *Señora* (Mrs.), or *Señorita* (Miss), followed by the first family name. Older and highly respected people are often greeted with *Don* or *Doña* followed by their first name, for example: Don Juan Carlos.

Traditional Mexican families were large. The father was the leader and provider. The mother was responsible for keeping the home and raising the children. This arrangement can still be found in some rural areas. Today, however, 75 percent of Mexico's people live in cities. Women often work, and families are much smaller. In rural Mexico, divorce was almost unknown. In the city, however, it is becoming more common.

MEXICAN CULTURE TODAY

Since the arrival of the Spaniards nearly 500 years ago, Mexican culture has undergone constant change. Today, the country has a broad range of lifestyles. Small pockets of isolated people continue to live in ways very similar to those of their ancestors hundreds of years ago. Most Mexicans, however, have entered a "modern age." Their language, religion, diet, and some customs may be different from those of many Northern Americans, but their desire to make a good living, to educate their children, and to have a comfortable and secure home is strong. So too is their belief in Christianity, democracy, equal protection under the law, and upward social mobility. Americans, Canadians, and Mexicans may be different, but they are alike in so many ways—including all of the ways that are most important.

Sandy beaches, a tropical climate, and the sparkling water of the Caribbean Sea attract millions of tourists to Cancún each year. This splendid physical site is but one of many strengths—natural, historical, and cultural—upon which Mexico can draw as the country attempts to build its economy further and improve the living standards of its 113 million people.

9

Mexico Looks Ahead

By nearly any measure, Mexico should have a bright and prosperous future. It has an abundance of human and natural resources, both of which are essential to economic growth and development. Spatially, it lies next door to the world's economic giant, the United States. But as you have seen, there are also many factors that can stand in the way of gaining stability and prosperity, and achieving a better life for its people. This final chapter reviews Mexico's strengths and weaknesses and concludes with a gaze into the crystal ball, hoping to see what its future may bring.

To understand the present, we must look to the past. A backward glance in time is not always pleasant. A massive imbalance in wealth and power has marked Mexican society during the 500 years of Spanish cultural dominance. Political, economic, and social conditions, for the most part, have always been unstable and unequal. These conditions continue to plague various segments of Mexican society. But generally speaking, more people are better off today than at any time in the country's history. And there are many reasons to be optimistic about the future.

For the first time in the five centuries since the Spanish conquest, Mexico has a truly democratic government. The country's once unsustainable rate of population growth is in sharp decline. In a single generation (about 30 years), the number of children in each family has dropped from nearly seven to just over three. This allows the country's economy to catch up with population growth. After nearly a decade of economic stagnation, there are signs that Mexico's economy has reached what economists call the "take-off stage" of accelerated growth. The country has a rich store of natural resources, including large deposits of petroleum and natural gas that can help fuel further economic development. It also has a wealth of metals. Nature, culture, and history have generously combined to make Mexico an ideal destination for tourists. Perhaps the most important resource of all is the country's 113 million people. They are hardworking, have strong family ties, and are increasingly well educated.

Mexico, however, also continues to have problems. The country has long suffered from bad government and widespread corruption in both business and politics. Certainly these barriers to stability and development will continue to present challenges. Broad gaps in income, opportunity, and power have caused considerable civil unrest. Mexico must work to ensure that all of its people are included in the country's expanding democracy and economy. Environmental pollution must be curtailed. The country's infrastructure—its highways, railroads, and communications systems, and the distribution of clean water and energy—must be vastly improved. The drug trade presents both Mexicans and Anglo-Americans with a host of critical issues that must be addressed. And the outflow of migrants into the United States is a thorny issue on both sides of the border.

NAFTA and the maquiladora program continue to link Mexico's economy very closely to that of the United States. As the American economy suffered a sharp downturn during the first decade of the twenty-first century, Mexico's economy also suffered a major slump. One huge problem Mexico faces is growing competition from cheaper labor in China and elsewhere in south and east Asia. Many American and Canadian companies find it less costly to outsource manufacturing to Asia than it is to pay rising Mexican wages. Their work has been transferred to distant lands across the Pacific. As a result, during the past decade hundreds of maquiladoras have closed. (A good lesson in the geography of manufacturing can be learned in any large discount store. How many goods are "Made in Mexico" versus those "Made in China"?) Although Mexico's 2010 unemployment rate of about 6 percent is relatively low when compared to that of the twentieth century, it is a full point higher than that of a decade ago. And underemployment remains high, at about 25 percent of the working population.

If Mexico is to prosper, it must do three things. First, it must make certain that the new commitment to democracy and political stability continues to grow. Second, corruption must be weeded out and criminal activity, particularly the drug trade and growing power of the drug cartels, must be curtailed. Finally, the country's economy must continue to grow, and its benefits must reach all segments of Mexican society. There are many signs that Mexico is on the brink of achieving these goals and finally realizing its full potential. *¡Viva Mexico!*

Country Name	United Mexican States (Estados Unidos Mexicanos) Conventional: Mexico
Location	North America; largest country within Middle America; between the United States and Guatemala and Belize; facing Pacific Ocean to the west and the Gulf of Mexico and Caribbean Sea to the east
Area	761,606 square miles (1,972,550 square kilometers)
Capital	Mexico City
Climate	Wet tropical to desert; much of the climate is influenced by elevation, rather than latitude
Terrain	Low coastal plains, particularly on the Gulf coast and Yucatán Peninsula; high, rugged mountains, separated by high, arid plateau in the north and central regions
Elevation Extremes	Lowest point, Laguna Salada, 33 feet (10 meters) below sea level; Highest point, Mount Orizaba (volcano), 18,406 feet (5,610 meters)
Natural Hazards	Volcanic eruptions and earthquakes in the south; tsunamis along the Pacific coast; hurricanes on the Gulf of Mexico and Caribbean coasts; flooding in low-lying areas and stream valleys
Land Use	Arable land: 12 percent; permanent crops: 1 percent; pastureland: 39 percent; forest and woodland: 26 percent; urban and wasteland: 22 percent
Environmental Issues	Water scarce and polluted in north; inaccessible and of poor quality in the center and southeast; general pollution in urban areas; water pollution in urban areas; deforestation; desertification; erosion in upland areas; air pollution in Mexico City and urban centers along the U.S.–Mexico border
Population	113 million (July 2010 estimate)
Population Growth Rate	1.1 percent per year (July 2010 estimate; declining)
Life Expectancy	76 years (male, 73 years; female, 79 years)
Nationality	Mexican(s)
Ethnic Groups	Mestizo (Amerindian-Spanish), 60 percent; Amerindian or predominantly Amerindian, 30 percent; white (European), 9 percent; other, 1 percent
Religions	Roman Catholic, 76 percent; Protestant, 6 percent; other, 14 percent; none, 4 percent

124

Languages	Spanish; various Mayan, Nahuatl, and other native languages
Literacy	95 percent
Type of Government	Federal republic
Head of State	President
Independence	September 16, 1810 (from Spain)
Administrative Divisions	31 states and 1 federal district
Flag Description	Three equal vertical bands of green, white, and red; the coat of arms (an eagle perched on a cactus with a snake in its beak) is centered in the white band
Currency	Mexican peso
Gross Domestic Product	$1.482 billion (2009 est.); averages twelfth-ranking position among world economies
Labor Force by Occupation	Services, 63 percent; industry, 23 percent; agriculture, 14 percent
Industries	Food and beverage, tobacco, chemicals, iron and steel, petroleum, mining, textiles, clothing, motor vehicles, consumer durables, tourism
Exports	($230 billion, 2009 est.) Manufactured goods, oil and oil products, silver, fruits and vegetables, coffee, cotton; approximately 80 percent of all export trade is with the United States
Imports	($234 billion, 2009 est.) Metalworking machines, steel products, agricultural machinery, electrical equipment, vehicle parts for assembly, parts for vehicle repair; 48 percent of all imports are from the United States
Transportation	Highways: 222,000 miles (357,000 kilometers), of which 111,000 miles (178,000 kilometers) are paved; railways: 11,200 miles (18,000 kilometers); airports: 1,744 (246 with paved runways)

B.C.	
ca. 20,000	Earliest evidence of humans in Mexico.
ca. 7000	Earliest evidence of plant domestication and deliberate planting of crops.
ca. 5000	Maize cultivation and earliest evidence of permanent settlements.
3000–2500	Agricultural villages; advanced farming methods; refinement of tools, weapons, and crafts; foundations of later civilizations.
1500–400	Olmec culture thrives.
1100	Early Mayan culture appears.
A.D.	
200	Decline of Olmec culture; beginning of the city of Teotihuacán.
400	Emergence of classic period of Mayan civilization.
650	Collapse of Teotihuacán.
800–900	Decline of Mayan civilization.
1300	Beginning of Chichimec invasions from the north.
1325	Founding of the Aztec capital, Tenochtitlán, on the site of present-day Mexico City.
1400–1519	Aztec empire expands and grows in strength.
1492	Christopher Columbus reaches the Caribbean.
1519	Hernán Cortés, with 11 ships, 100 sailors, and 508 soldiers, arrives on the Gulf coast of Mexico.
1521	Cortés captures Aztec capital of Tenochtitlán and destroys city, effectively ending the Aztec civilization.
1522	Cortés selects site of Tenochtitlán for his capital, Mexico City.
1531	Juan Diego, an Indian living in Guadeloupe, claims to have seen the Virgin Mary. The dark-skinned "Virgin of Guadeloupe" became Mexico's patron saint.
1530–1600	Period of exploration and gradual expansion to occupy territory now controlled by Mexico and into what is now the southwestern United States.
1546	Silver discovered in Zacatecas, drawing thousands of Spaniards into the area; beginning of silver boom.
1551	First university in the Western Hemisphere established in Mexico City.
1550–1650	The "silver era," during which Mexico's silver mines produced vast wealth that supported Spain's economy.

1610–1750	Territorial expansion into what is now the United States.
1810	Mexico declares independence from Spain.
1810–1821	War of Independence.
1830s	Growing tensions between the United States and Mexico.
1836	Santa Anna battles American rebels at the Alamo in San Antonio. All Americans are killed, but several weeks later Santa Anna's troops are defeated at San Jacinto by General Sam Houston, and Santa Anna is taken prisoner.
1845	United States annexes Texas.
1846–1848	War between Mexico and America. After Mexico's defeat, the United States pays $15 million for a huge area that is now roughly the southwestern quarter of the United States.
1876–1811	Period of Porfirio Díaz leadership; a time of relative peace and modernization.
1910–1920	Mexican Revolution; bloodiest period in independent Mexico's history.
1917	Adoption of Mexico's current constitution; Partido Revolucionario Institucional (PRI political party) formed.
1929	PRI elected to lead country, a position it held until voted out of office in 2000.
1968	Summer Olympics held in Mexico City.
1976	Huge oil reserves discovered in southeastern Mexico bordering on and in the Bay of Campeche.
1985	Major earthquake strikes Mexico City, resulting in many deaths and great property loss.
1994	North American Free Trade Agreement (NAFTA) implemented; beginning of guerrilla uprising in Chiapas by Zapatista Liberation Army.
2000	Vicente Fox, of the National Action Party (PAN), wins presidential election, ending 71 years of PRI control.
2006	Conservative PAN candidate Felipe Calderon wins presidential election by a very thin margin; President Calderon announces a stepped-up war on drugs.
2007	Mexican Carlos Slim overtakes Microsoft founder Bill Gates to become world's wealthiest person.

2010   Amid growing American concerns over illegal migrants, the state of Arizona passes controversial illegal immigration enforcement bill; U.S. president Barack Obama announces plans to send 1,200 National Guard troops to help secure U.S.–Mexico border.

Baedeker Travel Guide. *Mexico*. New York: Macmillan Travel, Simon & Schuster Macmillan, 2008.

Casagrande, Louis B., and S.A. Johnson. *Focus on Mexico: Modern Life in an Ancient Land*. Minneapolis: Lerner Publications Co., 1986.

Eyewitness Travel Guide. *Mexico*. London: Dorling Kindersley Limited, 2003.

Gilbert, M. Joseph, and T.J. Henderson, eds. *The Mexico Reader: History, Culture, Politics*. Durham, N.C.: Duke University Press, 2002.

Merrill, Tim, ed. *Mexico*. A Country Study, Area Handbook Series, Library of Congress. Washington, D.C.: U.S. Government Printing Office, 1997.

Noble, John, et al. *Mexico*. Oakland, Calif: Lonely Planet Publications, 2010.

Stein, R. Conrad. *Mexico*. New York: Children's Press, 1998.

Web sites

About.Com: Geography
http://geography.about.com

Central Intelligence Agency. CIA—The World Factbook, Mexico
https://www.cia.gov/library/publications/the-world-factbook/geos/mx.html

Consulate General of Mexico
http://www.mexico-info.com

CountryReports: Mexico
http://www.countryreports.org/country.aspx?countryid=160&countryName= Mexico

The MEXonline Guide to Mexico
http://www.mexonline.com

NationMaster.com
http://www.nationmaster.com/index.php

U.S. Library of Congress Country Studies: Mexico
http://lcweb2.loc.gov/frd/cs/mxtoc.html

U.S. Department of State: Background Notes
http://www.state.gov/p/wha/ci/mx

Picture Credits

Index

Index

CHARLES F. "FRITZ" GRITZNER is Distinguished Professor Emeritus of Geography at South Dakota State University in Brookings. In 2010, he retired from teaching after a 50-year career of college teaching. In retirement, Fritz, his wife, Yvonne, and their "family" of two Italian greyhounds remain in South Dakota. He enjoys travel, writing, and sharing his love for geography with readers. As a senior consulting editor and frequent author for Chelsea House Publishers' MODERN WORLD NATIONS, MAJOR WORLD CULTURES, EXTREME ENVIRONMENTS, and GLOBAL CONNECTIONS series, Fritz has a wonderful opportunity to combine each of these "hobbies." Dr. Gritzner has served as both president and executive director of the National Council for Geographic Education (NCGE) and has received the council's highest honor, the George J. Miller Award for Distinguished Service to Geographic Education, as well as numerous other national teaching, service, and research recognitions from the NCGE, the Association of American Geographers, and other organizations.